NEWSMAN

PAT COLLINS

Available at:
Politics and Prose Bookstore
5015 Connecticut Ave. NW
Washington, D.C. 20008
www.politics-prose.com / / (202) 364-1919

To

Emily Bender Collins
Mother of three
Grandmother of five
Wife extraordinaire

INTRODUCTION

"WHAT DO YOU MAKE OF IT?" It's a signature question of mine. Why? Because you can't answer that question with a yes or no. You have to say something. Something meaningful, I hope.

In the world of television, we call that a sound bite. At a scene when I meet someone who saw something," What do you make of it?" is my go-to question. I was going to name this book What Do You Make of It? but then I thought critics might read it and say," Not much."

Welcome to my storybook.

My name is Pat Collins. I'm a fourth-generation Washingtonian. My children are fifth generation and my grandchildren sixth generation. I have been a reporter at:

The Washington Daily News

The Washington Star

Channel 9 News

Channel 7 News

Channel 4 News

I have been on television for more than 46 years and during that time I have covered thousands of stories in and around the city of Washington. My career has morphed into basically two things: I cover murders, and I measure snow. But there have been some other interesting assignments, as well.

Read now about some of my adventures and some of the people I have met along the way.

NEWSMAN

PAT COLLINS

LIFE PRIOR TO MY LIFE IN THE NEWS

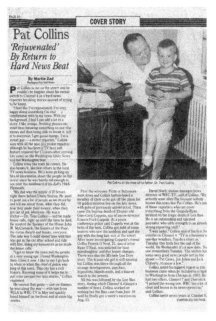

On Father's knee

H STREET

It was almost like clockwork—7:15 AM. We would be eating breakfast and out our dining-room window we would see her at her second-floor window with a bucket in her hand.

Mayola Jones had no plumbing, so each morning she would toss her nighttime deposits down into the yard below. Out our window my father would yell, "Good morning, Mayola," and sometimes she would look up and wave. Mayola wasn't embarrassed. It was the way she did her daily business.

Mayola Jones was a fixture on H Street. She had a Brunhilda-like appearance—a prominent nose, flowing clothes, little tufts of hair here and there. She lived by herself in a house down an alley – all alone. No one knew exactly where she came from or why she was there or how she got there. But she had been there a long time.

As best I can determine, Mayola did two things to make a living. She stepped in front of DC Transit buses and then sued the bus system's owner, O. Roy Chalk. In between 'accidents,' she would be a featured invalid at faith-healing revivals under a tent down off Benning Road.

Mayola would hobble up on the stage with her crutches. The reverend, in a white, sweat-stained shirt with a Bible tucked under his arm, would renounce the Devil, call down the power of God, and ceremoniously touch Mayola on the forehead. Mayola would fall to the ground. Down went the crutches. Up came Mayola.

"Healed!" she would cry out. "Healed!" And then triumphantly leave the stage.

Another H Street miracle.

Crutches were part of Mayola's wardrobe. She had them at the ready at all times. Limping along in an awkward cadence down the street until—well, until she hit the alley path to her home. Then she would lift those crutches like wings and in a fast jog make her way into her house, safe—and saved—once again. God is good.

H Street, Northeast, was the place where I grew up, a fourth-generation Washingtonian. 324 H Street; phone number Lincoln 3-0772. It was the place where my father grew up—and his father, my grandfather, a railroad engineer. It was a row house about three blocks from Union Station. My grandfather could walk to Union Station from home.

The railroad was the economic engine that powered H Street. Railroad workers, many of them Irish, lived there. They called the neighborhood Swamp Poodle. I'm still not sure how they came up with that name. Merchants lived above their stores. There was a European feel about the place. There was a meat man, an ice man, a milk man, a vegetable man – they worked the alleys and sold their goods from carts. It was a cash-and-carry world, but they would carry you until payday if cash was short.

For a time, H Street was one of the busiest streets in the city of Washington. But it was never a lace-curtain kind of life. Just a lot of everyday people doing what they could.

My father worked his way through Catholic University, then Georgetown University Medical School. He met my mother while he was doing his residency at DC General. Her name was Nellie Salley. She was from South Carolina and came to Washington on a special government program. The deal went something like this: We'll pay for your nursing education if you stay on and work in public health. It turned out to be quite a bargain. It got her a good education and a trip north—and she never looked back.

My father was a general practitioner. Today we call them internists. Back then, general practitioners would do a variety of medical procedures including birthing babies. My father said some mothers were so happy and excited that they named their babies after him. So ,if there is a Tom Collins in your family, now you know why.

Back then, as they do now, people would often call each other by their last names. my mother was known as Salley, first in the hospital, then in her personal life. And then, after she was married, it became Salley Collins.

I keep saying,"Back then," because things were much different *back then*. There was no air conditioning. Cars came mostly in one color: black. People tuned in to radios to get the latest news and information.

The big newspaper back then was The Evening Star – a red stripe on the front page signaling the final edition with stocks and sports reports. My father would give me change each night and I would run to the liquor store across the street and get him the Red Stripe. He would lean back in his leather recliner, open the paper, and catch up on the day's news. When he was settled in, often I would run and jump into that paper and try to scare him. That sudden move would spark all kinds of feelings from my father—feigned fear, some anger, and occasionally a good laugh.

I still remember some of my favorite stores on H Street:

High's at Fourth and H. Ice cream, a nickel a scoop, five-scoop cone for a quarter.

Love's Toy Store. Mr. Love was ever so patient as I roamed the store looking for that perfect toy.

Benny's grocery store. No money, no problem— you could pay later.

5th and H. They called it Toyland, but it sold all kinds of things. One day I bought a plug of chewing tobacco and took it home. My grandmother wanted to try some, too. My mouth caught fire, and she coughed so much she spit out her false teeth.

Sam's Dry Cleaners. Sam's had calendars with pinup girls – no one had to ask me twice to pick up the cleaning.

McBride's. A big-time five-and-dime. This was our version of the Dollar Store, except better. It sold everything, including canaries and dyed baby chickens at Easter.

Morton's. A walking-distance department store for those who didn't want to pay downtown prices.

Miles Long. This was the City's place for cheesesteaks and some of the thickest chocolate shakes – you needed a spoon to eat one.

When I was a little boy, the boundary was Fourth Street. Then Sixth Street. Then Eighth Street. When I turned 13 – freedom!

My father opened an office on the first floor of the row house adjoining the old Collins house, his family home, which then became the headquarters for the Visiting Nurses. We lived on the second floor of the two adjoined homes. There were a lot of narrow twists and turns upstairs, but it all worked out.

My mother ran my father's office. I was the youngest of four children. My real name was Joseph Patrick Collins, but I was such a fat baby that my siblings called me Fatty Patty, and the Pat part stuck. Unfortunately, so did some of the fat.

I was raised by an African American woman. We called her Cora Roland Collins King. While my mom was working in the office, Cora watched after my brother, sisters, and me. She cooked and cleaned and kept us out of trouble. Cora was family. If I were particularly bad, Cora would transform herself into her alter ego, take off her glasses, and become "Mabel"— and lay down the law. I never wanted to mess with "Mabel."

My father had an eclectic group of patients: politicians (Democrats and Republicans), clergy (priests, bishops, even the cardinal), government workers, Little Sisters of the Poor, tradesmen. My favorite of all his patients: performers from the Ringling Brothers and Barnum & Bailey Circus. When the circus was in town he would close his office and treat the performers. I saw the Fish Man, the Tattoo Lady, the midgets, and the clowns. It was like having my own personal sideshow right there in my living room.

A few years ago, I ran across some of my father's books. He charged five dollars for an office visit. Sometimes he worked for barter. He treated a patient for some disease or condition, and a few weeks later we had a new sink or a paint job in the hallway. My father charged seven dollars for a house call. After dinner he would get in his 1946 Plymouth coupe and go from home to home to visit the sick. Oftentimes I would ride along and do my homework in the car while he tended to the patient.

As we drove from place to place, my father would point to various spots in the City and tell me stories. I remember his calling Washington "a city of magnificent distances," drawing people seeking success from all over the world.

My father was always busy. Getting one-on-one time with him was special. House-call moments meant a lot to me—even the time he was called to visit an unconscious patient at his workshop. It was dark, and for some reason I went in with my dad. The man was dead. I watched my father try to take his pulse. Nothing there. I was about nine. It was the first time I saw death in person. My mother wasn't happy about that, but for me it was sort of a macabre adventure.

My father was a good doctor, a great diagnostician. But he was a tough parent. In my father's world, if you weren't working you were goofing off, and if you were goofing off he wanted nothing to do with you. I have his sayings memorized:

- "Be alert to your surroundings."
- "Don't get caught in dreamy adolescence."
- "Don't be a victim of the Hobbity Hoy Stage of awkward adolescent mischief and misgivings."

He was a hard man who grew up in a hard way. I always tried to do things to make my father proud of me, but it didn't always work out. I still get flashbacks of times with my father. I remember once at the dinner table we were eating watermelon for dessert. My father cracked some joke. My mother said, "Okay, kids, let's get him," and she pretended to heave her watermelon slice at my dad. She pretended—but I followed through and hit him point blank in the face. The juices ran down his shirt. He was stunned. I was scared. My mother intervened.

I remember the time I said the word "fuck" in front of my father. I was trying to start a power lawn mower. I yanked hard on the starter cord. It snapped in two. I fell backward. Out came the "Fuuuck," and my father just stood there, red-faced. He didn't say a word. He didn't have to. I could swear there was steam coming out of his ears. I never said that word in front of him ever again.

One of the things my father did was treat and care for the Gonzaga High School football team. Gonzaga was just a few blocks from our house. It was a Jesuit-run school, and my father had a very close relationship with the Jesuits. My father sat on the bench during the games; most of the time he took me along. The players looked like Goliaths to me as I saw them run on and off the field.

My father was a strict Catholic, my mother a convert. We said the rosary on our knees every night. There was not a lot of freedom of choice in our house. When it came time for high school, Gonzaga was not in the conversation. You see, my father went to St. John's College High School, and my brother did, too. So even though I could walk to Gonzaga, I took two buses and a streetcar across town to St. John's. No questions asked. Young Catholic teenager, all-boys military school, which brings me to sex.....

SEX

In virtually every manual on how to be a parent, in every corny documentary about raising children, the experts say, "Talk to your kid about sex." But we know how it really works. Teenage boys learn about sex from movies and magazines and from talking to other teenage boys. Sex is the mysterious, forbidden fruit. The female form is most alluring – it's why guys watch girls in bikinis. It's sex, and it has magical, magnetic powers.

All of this explains why I went to Baltimore. When I was a teenager old enough to drive but too young to go to bars, my friend Bill and I decided to explore the world of sex in Baltimore, a port city about 30 miles north of Washington.

Baltimore has a harbor.

Baltimore has the Orioles.

Baltimore has Little Italy.

Baltimore has the Block.

The Board of Trade will gladly tell you about the harbor, the O's, and Little Italy. You learn about the Block from your buddies. It's a series of strip joints and sex shops not far from the police headquarters. It was the home of the Two O'clock Club and world-class stripper Blaze Starr. Movies were made about her. Along the street, barkers would stand outside and lure you in with promises of passion inside these dark – really dark – dens of pleasure: "We have the best dancers, the prettiest performers – our girls do things you have never experienced before." There was a carny-like atmosphere on the street as knots of people moved from place to place.

For many teenage boys the Baltimore Block was a secret Saturday night destination. At least it was for me. So one night I took my older brother's ID, gave my parents the movie alibi, joined my friend Bill, and the two of us were Baltimore-bound.

I had some rules:

- Don't get ripped off. To keep from getting robbed, I carefully folded a twenty-dollar bill and inserted it into the band of my right sock.
- Act sophisticated. Don't fall victim to the promises of barkers.
- Look for the best beer deal.

We watched dances by girls with names like Cookie, Ginger, and Dawn. Exercising some willpower, we managed to make it through the evening tipping but not touching. Just think about baseball. . . .

Towards the end of the night things got hotter. A lot hotter. Downright steamy for a teenage boy on the prowl. It happened late, when my pockets were just about empty, and we were making plans to head back to Washington. There was this building—well, it really wasn't a building, it was a tiny, narrow place shoehorned in between two buildings, and it was set back from the other places on the block.

There was a door, and beside the door a large plate-glass window, and behind the plate-glass window a small round table with a chair. And in that chair sat a beautiful young lady. She had dark hair, doe-like eyes and a thin but inviting smile. She was totally different from the harsh painted ladies we had seen on the Block. She was innocent. And did I mention inviting?

I told my friend Bill, "Just give me a minute," and in the door I went, and once inside I said something clever, like, "Hey, what's going on in here?"

She said, "Do you want to have some gypsy fun?"

I said, "Me? Yes." I said, "Yes."

The beautiful young woman said, "Twenty bucks—but it will be worth it."

Twenty dollars, twenty dollars—now where would I come up with twenty dollars?

Well, you know where. Without trying to look like too much of a dork, I pretended to scratch my leg, not so subtly slipped two fingers into my right sock, and extracted the twenty-dollar bill – my emergency money. By now my palms were sweating. I anxiously placed the wadded-up bill into her delicate hands. Did I mention they were inviting hands?

Once she had the money she went to the front of the store and pulled the curtain over the plate-glass window, blocking the view from the street. It was getting steamy now.

The beautiful young woman said, "I'll be back in a minute," then disappeared behind yet another curtain that reached from floor to ceiling behind that table, behind that chair. So there I stood in a high state of anticipation, sandwiched between two brightly colored curtains, all sorts of possibilities racing through my mind.

When will she come back?

What will she be wearing?

What will she do?

It was lonely standing there between two big curtains with all those things on your mind. I shifted from one foot to the other, waiting and waiting. I wanted gypsy fun – and I wanted it now.

Well, I got it.

In a flash, the beautiful young woman came bursting through the curtain, hands in the air, fingers snapping high above her head, behind her this linebacker-sized man with a leather vest and violin in hand. As he played, she danced circles around me, bounding and hopping and snapping those fingers. I was dizzy just watching her.

Two minutes later the music stopped. She grabbed both my hands and, looking directly in my eyes, said, "Now you've had gypsy fun!"

I looked at the big man with the violin. I looked at the beautiful woman. I looked like a fool. I left that little storefront, tracked down my friend Bill, and headed back to Washington. Good thing we started out with a full tank of gas.

A CAREER CHANGER—BEFORE THE CAREER

Summer in the city of Washington gets hot, sizzling hot. We had no air-conditioning. My brother and I shared a room that had a window fan. Night after summer night we would lie still in bed listening to the Senators game on the radio, trying to catch a breeze. Trying to steal some sleep. We got relief at Bay Ridge, a summer-place community on the Chesapeake Bay. My father bought a parcel of land and built a house there, and we escaped as often as we could.

It was there one summer night that my life took a turn that had career consequences. I was a junior in high school, sitting on the front porch, writing those dreaded summer book reports. My sister had a date. She was late getting ready. Her date killed time by reading my reports. "You're a pretty good writer," he said. "How would you like to cover high-school sports for the Washington Daily News?" My sister's date was not some random guy; he was George Clifford, the sports columnist for the Daily News. I thought he was just blowing smoke, but I got that job, and by my senior year I was editing three pages of high school sports and writing a column as well.

The Daily News took chances with me. I knew nothing about golf, but the editors said neither do most of the readers, so they sent me out to cover big-time golfers. I had exclusive one-on-ones with Arnold Palmer and Gary Player. Great golfers. Great gentlemen. Great interviews. At the time, I didn't know the difference between a 9-iron and a sand wedge. But it didn't matter—their stories were bigger than the game.

It was at the Daily News that I learned to write. Crusty old newspapermen would throw copy back to me and make me write it, rewrite it, and then write it again until it was, well, just right. "Read it aloud," they would say. When a story is well written and you read it out loud, it sings. Writing and reporting, putting a newspaper together, became addictive. There was so much action at the paper that I never wanted to leave because, if I left, I might just miss something.

At home I found a different sentiment.

My father didn't want me to become a reporter. He said reporters were nothing more than a bunch of drifters, deadbeats, and drunks. He said he knew because some of them were his patients. Somewhere it's written that if your father is a doctor, you are destined to be one too. My father wanted ever so badly for me to be a doctor. Soooo, before I left for college, I promised him I would put the newspaper stuff aside, major in biology, and study to become a doctor, just like he did.

My father said I could go to any college I could get into as long as it was Catholic. He made one exception: the Johns Hopkins University in Baltimore. It had a special medical program: three years undergrad, then medical school and the M.D. degree. The thought of my being a Johns Hopkins doctor made my dad smile. As it turns out, I was wait-listed at Johns Hopkins but accepted at the University of Notre Dame. So Notre Dame it would be. It satisfied my father's requirement; it was Catholic. More importantly, it satisfied my requirement: it was in South Bend, Indiana – miles away from my father and his rules.

Three months after arriving at Notre Dame, I started an underground paper, The Whisper a take-off on The Voice the school's official paper. I used my own money to do it. Then I decided to change my major to English.

The summer after my freshman year I had a come-to-Jesus moment with my father. I told him that I had decided to major in English, which meant I wouldn't be following in his medical doctor footsteps. He didn't take it well.

My father was a tough guy with strict rules and severe penalties – or at least threats of severe penalties. I'll give you an example of the type of punishment my father meted out when he was displeased. My parents bought my older sister Mary a beaver jacket. Mary loved that jacket, and she looked wonderful in it. Every time my father caught Mary smoking a cigarette, he took her jacket away. That jacket went back and forth, back and forth. That poor beaver had to have been dizzy from it all. I tell you this just to give you some insight into our house rules.

After I delivered my career change news to my father, I expected the worst. I didn't have a beaver coat, so that wasn't in jeopardy. First my father accused me of losing my religion, then losing my good sense. I think there was a little inheritance talk thrown in as well.

Needless to say, it was a rough summer, with me doing my best to avoid family dinners and clashes. But eventually, with some intercession by my sainted mother, he accepted my new path. I have since learned that parents are resilient, and that they can never quit or be fired from their jobs of mother and father.

TEEN ANGEL

That's what my friends jokingly called her. She was my first true love. And then she disappeared. Vanished.

First, a quick reminder: Notre Dame was an all-boys school with a long list of campus rules – and an equally long list of student strategies to avoid them.

Lights out. Stuff blanket in glass transom to give the appearance of darkness.

Curfew. Go to bathroom, punch out screen, and jump to freedom.

Mandatory Mass. Sign in and duck out.

Dress for dinner. Coat and tie required – same coat, same tie, same T-shirt.

I was a sophomore when I met her in the basement of the student center. There, guys mingled with girls and occasionally danced to the music on the jukebox. I'm not going to say her name because I don't know what happened or where she is today. I can't stand a story without an ending, and this story doesn't have one. My classmates joked and teased me, calling her Teen Angel. For the purpose of the story, we'll just call her T. A.

T.A. was cute, and she could dance—and kiss—and one thing led to another. And another. We couldn't keep our hands off each other. I'll let you fill in the blanks. She was from a well-to-do family in Chicago. They sent the family chauffeur to take us out on dates. I was in college, going to rugby parties and smokers in a chauffeur-driven limo. I was in heaven right there at the Golden Dome. T.A. wrote the steamiest letters. I read them and reread them until I had them memorized. I was in LOVE.

Then a couple of things – a couple of people – derailed my relationship with my T.A.

First, the chauffeur. I suspect that the chauffeur told his boss that things were getting too serious between T.A. and me and that this bit of news did not make the boss happy. Next, my mother. Mother intercepted one of T.A.'s love letters. It did not make her happy. Then – poof – when I returned to Notre Dame after break, my T.A. was gone. Long gone. There were no calls. There were no cards. There were no letters. Nothing. EVER.

It was right about then that my father started calling me the "Prince of Pleasure." It stuck. I even had a T-shirt with my new title on it.

WRITE AWAY

At Notre Dame I got involved in The Scholastic, a weekly Time-like magazine. Then some other students and I founded The Observer. It was somewhat of a coup. You see, Notre Dame had a newspaper called The Voice. It came out every now and then and was something less than a must read on campus. The Voice was crippled by antiquated printing techniques and a severe lack of funds. A revolution was in order. Remember, this was the '60s, the age of rebellion. "Don't trust anybody over 30." Us against them. A group of students – Robert Sam Anson, Ken Socha, Steve Feldhaus, some other students, and I – plotted to kill The Voice. The Voice's final edition, with the headline "The Voice is Dead," was probably the sad little paper's most well-read edition. A few weeks later we came back with something brand new: The Observer. It was sharp, sassy, and independent.

We financed it through student subscription fees and ads that we sold ourselves. We saved money by having students do all the pre-press production work. Why, we even paid salaries. Not much – maybe cigarette money – but salaries, nonetheless. A real newspaper had to be published more than just every now and then, and The Observer was, and is, a real newspaper. We started publishing twice a week, then three times a week; within a year or so it was a daily.

The Observer became a must-read on the Notre Dame campus, but that didn't make us popular with University "management." One time we used the word "screw" in a story and caught hell for that. "Smut" on Our Lady's face, some alumni wrote. There was hell to pay, but we kept on printing.

Then, to make extra money, we came out with Saturday game-day sports specials. Names and numbers of the players, stories about the game, all for 10 cents. Seems harmless, right? Not really. We were in direct competition with the official slick Notre Dame football game day program – price two bucks – and we were cutting into Notre Dame's profits. The school moved my vendors off campus. Way off. By the end, they weren't even in the same zip code as the Notre Dame stadium.

In spite of the setbacks, The Observer kept plugging along. Over the years it has produced many notable reporters, editors, and even a couple of Pulitzer Prize winners. Being a founder of and reporter at The Observer are among the most significant things I've ever done. Certainly, working on The Observer was one of my best experiences.

Class? I went to class sometimes. Remember that I was an English major – an 18th-century English major. We studied only about five authors and a dozen books. Find a comfortable chair and start reading. No problem.

In addition to working on The Observer, I filed stories for Newsweek magazine and the Washington Daily News. There were two things in play back then. First, Notre Dame football. It was the Ara Parseghian years, and the team was strong and more popular than ever. Then there was the Pentecostal movement. a group of uber-religious followers. They met in the basement of the Administration Building and prayed. They prayed real hard – so hard that they began to talk in tongues – words that sounded like Greek or Latin or Arabic. No one was quite sure. But it was a fascinating phenomenon. Newsweek couldn't get enough of it. It ruined some of my Friday nights, but it was an intriguing story. And the money came in handy.

HERO TODAY, GONE TOMORROW

In the '60s Jimmy Breslin was big in the newspaper business. He had a must-read daily column in New York City, and he authored a popular book, *The Gang That Couldn't Shoot Straight*. Everybody talked to and about Jimmy Breslin. My God, he was a pen pal of the serial killer Son of Sam.

I loved Jimmy Breslin. I wanted to be just like Jimmy Breslin. I made it a point to read his newspaper column whenever I could.

Fast-forward to the University of Notre Dame on a crisp autumn day. There was football in the air. At Notre Dame football is always in the air, but this time was special. This was the week before the game of the century, Notre Dame versus Michigan State. A national championship was at stake, and though the game was to be played at East Lansing, the focus of attention the week before the game was the campus of Notre Dame.

Sports Illustrated came to Notre Dame.

Network television crews came to Notre Dame.

It seemed like a convention of writers and reporters.

Standing out amidst all the scribblers was Jimmy Breslin, Everyman's voice, and in my opinion, the best newspaper writer in the English-speaking world. (When you are young -- and I was young -- there is no middle ground on things; they are either terrific or terrible, and Jimmy was terrific.) Yikes! Did I just write something in parentheses? I hate parentheses.

I remember when I first saw him. He was sitting on a bench in the hallway of the Administration

Building beneath the famed Golden Dome. He had a tiny portable typewriter on his lap. His hair was tousled, his jacket rumpled, his focus intense. He would put a piece of paper in the typewriter, pound out several words, and then stop, read the words, rip the paper from the carriage, crumple it up, crank in another piece of paper, and do this over and over again until he got it just right.

For a young reporter, watching Breslin write was a valuable lesson. If this great writer could spend so much time finding the words to tell a story, how could I be satisfied spitting out some words and then just walk away? For Breslin, working a story was physical: He had short, strong fingers, and he struck the keys with such force and authority I thought the typewriter was going to fall apart.

I spent some time watching Breslin and his words and his typewriter in that grand Notre Dame hallway. I didn't approach him. I wouldn't do that. He was too intense. He was too important. Besides, I had my own reporting work to do.

This was a very big football game, and virtually every publication in the country wanted to have something to say about it. That would include the Washington Daily News. I wrote a campus color story for the Daily News. I would like to tell you that I struggled over every word just like Jimmy, but that's not the way it works. Sometimes you can learn something, but it takes years to put it into practice. For example, a golf swing.

Back in the '60s there was no Internet; there were no fax machines. The most effective way to transmit a story from one place to the other was Western Union.

If it seems like I'm stalling a bit here, it's because this is the part of the story that's hard to tell. That night I went to Western Union in downtown South Bend, and there was Jimmy Breslin. He was filing. I was filing. I felt big-time. Then he turned to me and said, "Hey, kid—know where I can get a drink around this place?" It was like a scene out of The Front Page. Jimmy Breslin talking to me, looking for drinking directions. Hey, honey, give me rewrite!

This happened late at night. In South Bend that meant about midnight. But I was connected, sort of. I had a number of side jobs at Notre Dame. One of them as a waiter at an Italian restaurant called Louie's, a pizza/pasta joint that sold beer by the quart. I never could understand that concept because there is simply no way you can finish a quart of beer before it gets warm although there were many nights we gave it the old college try.

I called Louie and explained, "There's a big-time newspaper writer in town, and he's looking for a beer. Can you keep the place open?" Louie thought about it for one second and said, "Of course."

This was really terrific drinking after hours with the great Jimmy Breslin in an Italian restaurant in the shadow of the Golden Dome. I needed a witness. I called a couple of friends. There was a speakeasy scene working there.

A knock on the door.

Louie answered.

We slipped inside.

Louie re-locked the door.

I had the feeling Louie had done this before.

My friends and I sat in the booth with Jimmy Breslin, quarts of beer lined up on the table before us. I don't know if it was the beer or my infatuation with Jimmy Breslin or both. We talked about this and that, and then I remember saying these words:

"You know what I like about you most, Mr. Breslin? I like the way you stand up for the common man, the everyday guy who plunks down change every morning to buy that paper."

"Yeah?" said Breslin. "You know what I think of that guy?"

"What, Mr. Breslin?"

"Fuck him, kid."

It wasn't the answer I expected.

A LOOK AT LIFE

In the '60s, magazines were still a big part of American culture. Time. Newsweek. Life. Their shiny pages and dramatic pictures were spread on cocktail tables in virtually every home in America. Look was one of those magazines. To get a feel for what young people were thinking, Look invited some college newspaper editors to Chicago for a sit-down round table. It went on for a couple of days. I went to a number of these gatherings and found them productive, if for no other reason than to share ideas on how to make our college newspapers better, more creative, and more independent.

At this gathering we talked politics. It came my turn. I said I wouldn't be surprised to see a Negro – that's the way we talked back then – president within my lifetime, and I would vote for him. Now that seemed like a simple, honest statement at the time, but to some back home it was downright inflammatory. Turns out I was right, and as promised I made that vote for Barack Obama.

BACK IN WASHINGTON

As time wore on, the railroads began to fail. The economic engine that powered H Street stalled. Sons and daughters of railroad people found other trades, other jobs. Some went off to college and became suited professionals. Many people moved to the suburbs in search of a carport, a barbecue pit, and some grass to cut. Others moved to avoid integration. When the railroad jobs left, crime moved in.

Through it all, my father stayed, but life on H Street was different. Our backyard was closed in with a six-foot-high chain-link fence topped with barbed wire. We had two watchdogs. They were stolen three times. It became a cottage industry to take the Collins' dogs, wait a few hours, knock on the door, and collect the reward. We had so many batteries stolen from our cars that my father used chains and locks to keep the hoods closed. We had a parking lot in the back of our house, if you came home late, getting from the alley to the front door could have you walking real fast. Sometimes running.

In April of my senior year at college came the riots. H Street was one of the targeted streets. Fires were set, stores looted. Heavy smoke filled the air. Rioters broke into my father's office and took drugs, typewriters, and equipment. My mother and father grabbed what they could, left their home, and, with my brother-in-law standing guard, made their way out of the neighborhood my father loved so much.

It was never the same after that. There was great tension in the air; buildings were bandaged with plywood; people were scared to buy; people were scared to sell. My parents moved to a high-rise in Hyattsville, Maryland. My father's office was downstairs and their makeshift home upstairs.

"H Street will come back," I remember him saying over and over and over. But not in his lifetime.

When I graduated from Notre Dame. I returned to Washington DC and began reporting for the Washington Daily News full time. I, too, lived in an apartment – my own apartment. When I got out of college, the last place I wanted to live was with my parents. Too many rules. Too many questions. It was time to start my life. On my own.

THE WASHINGTON DAILY NEWS

Young reporter at Daily News searching for the right word

NEWSPAPER PRESSES; NEWSROOMS

They start up slow and powerful, almost like a train engine – choo, choo, choo. When everything is aligned they go faster and faster and get louder and louder: CHOO, CHOO, CHOO. The building shakes. Papers spew out and pile up. There is a sense of excitement. It's like this gigantic metal machine is giving birth.

There is nothing quite like watching a newspaper press in action – especially if you have a story on the front page. It's damn near orgasmic.

Welcome to the Washington Daily News, 1013 13th Street, Northwest. Don't go looking for it today. I think the only thing left is a little plaque on a nondescript office building. In fact, when the Daily News building was around, it really wasn't much to look at: faux Colonial, red brick, three stories, shutters, an ancient elevator with a brass accordion safety gate and a jerky lifting mechanism that made you want to take the stairs.

The good, old newsrooms weren't supposed to look like hospitals or banquet halls. They were cluttered, dirty petri dishes of ideas, where questions were asked, obscenities shouted, objects thrown, and life's triumphs and tragedies recorded and memorialized—sometimes right next to a moldy ham sandwich left on a reporter's desk by some bastard – maybe the reporter himself.

The city desk: Last Supper long; heavy; sturdy. You could sleep on it, or maybe have sex on it. Along the side, wooden platforms with typewriters creating slots for editors and rewrite reporters. Over the big desk, hanging from the ceiling like large metal nostrils, pneumatic department-store tubes. They sucked the freshly typed and edited stories from the newsroom to the composing room a floor below – the stories written on cheap 8x10 paper, the pages glued with rubber cement, blue-penciled by an editor, rolled into a cylinder. Stuffed into the pneumatic tubes and then off to the printer. So much for the technical stuff.

THE REPORTERS

They came from all over. If it hadn't been for news-papers, these people probably would have never met. There were Ivy League grads, state-school grads, and no-school grads; frustrated poets and wannabe authors: Jews, Catholics, Protestants, and Seventh Day Adventists. You name it, they were there, and they all had one thing in common: They could tell a story that the reader would remember. At least for a little while. Here is a partial lineup of the *Washington Daily News* reporters:

Sam Stafford. Sam was a cigar-chomping, close-talking, hard-digging reporter. He once worked for the Sacramento Bee. A funny name for a paper, but it has quite a reputation.

Sam taught me two lessons. The first was 'Don't work scared.' He said when he first got into the business he was afraid of getting fired. Sometimes, he said, he wouldn't tackle stories—he would tiptoe through them. He said he felt like he was walking on a tightrope and there was a gigantic gorge beneath him. He wanted to be careful not to fall into the abyss. Then one day he got fired—pushed off the tightrope—only to find it was about four feet above the ground. He said he climbed back up on that rope and from then on he had an advantage over all the other reporters because he knew he could survive a fall.

Sam's second lesson was 'Know how to play the power players.' The editor of the Washington Daily News was a man by the name of Richard Hollander. He was rugged, handsome, barrel-chested, open-shirted.

Mr. Hollander – I still call him that – had been in Army Intelligence in World War II and had a commanding presence. He wasn't much for chit-chat. Mr. Hollander spent a lot of time in his office. It was not an office many reporters visited voluntarily.

Not so with Sam Stafford. You see, when Sam wanted to do a story, he visited Mr. Hollander in his office; Sam made sure we all knew he was going there. Sam would go into the office, exchange niceties with the boss, then come out, walk directly to the city editor, and tell him about the story he wanted to do. "I just saw the boss – it's got holy water on it." Bingo! Sam would get to do exactly what he wanted to do.

George Clifford. George was a reporter with a great sense of derring-do. He covered the Castro takeover of Cuba. He infiltrated and exposed the American Nazi party. He was a sports columnist, a political columnist. He could throw words like darts—or, if need be, daggers. He's the guy who got me into this business.

Johnny Burch never wrote a story in his entire life, but he was responsible for more front-page headlines than anyone else. There was a time when police headquarters were open and had pressrooms at which daily newspaper would station reporters. The reporters had free run of headquarters. They could go into the homicide squad room and read the detectives' reports as they were typing them, then run off to a phone for a whispered call to the paper. A rewrite reporter at the paper would put it all together with one of Johnny's headlines and then Page One.

Johnny didn't write much except his name on the back of a check but, boy, could his headlines grab your attention. He was to the Daily News what Ted Crowne was to the Washington Star and Al Lewis was to the Washington Post. All of them were little-known reporters responsible for big time stories. Ask Bob Woodward how the Post got tipped about Watergate.

Jerry Oppenheimer. Jerry was thin as a rail—a Richard Belzer kind of guy. He could work a phone better than anyone. Back then, each newsroom had a gigantic book called a crisscross. It allowed reporters to look up an address and then find the corresponding telephone number or vice versa. A reporter with a telephone number could find an address and find out who lived or worked there. If something really big had happened and the reporter had a deadline, he'd go to the crisscross and start dialing. Then start writing.

Louise Lague. She was elegant, and her writing had a light and airy feel to it. Louise graduated from Georgetown. She worked the Washington hoity-toity. Eventually she became a gossip columnist and then parlayed that into a job at People.

Joe Volz. Joe was a New Jersey guy who never met a conspiracy he didn't like or a crooked deal he didn't expose. He talked in an up-close, whispery way and wrote sharp, stinging stories using short words that would jab and leave a mark. Joe and I would often team up on stories. When the Daily News folded, Joe and I covered Watergate for the Star. We called our assignment "None of the President's Men."

David Holmberg. Holmberg's face looked like Ben Franklin's. His clothes looked like they came from an undertaker—you know, ash-gray suits, one size fits all. Holmberg was the Sultan of Sad. He did a lot of funerals. Tragedies. Stories that made a reader reach for a tissue.

Almost monthly Holmberg would quit, tell us he was done. Quitting was easy for Holmberg because he could put his entire life in the back of his compact car. He would pack his car and then unceremoniously drive north to Breezewood, Pennsylvania, a crossroad of interstate highways and a starting point for big trips west. There Holmberg would spend a night in a cheap motel and the next day he would drive back to DC and come back to the Daily News. About a month later he would quit all over again. For Holmberg, the Daily News was a journalistic Hotel California. Holmberg is a playwright in New York now.

Stan Felder. Stan was long-time city editor. He worked that slot for decades. Stan would find an overlooked story and guide a reporter in such a way to make that tiny little story big-time news. He could convince a reporter that the bank robbery down the street just might be the work of the next John Dillinger. Maybe. At least believing it at the time was a good-enough maybe to get you through the day..

Andy Beyer. Andy was a horse-racing specialist. He dropped out of Harvard to play the ponies. Andy sort of resembled a horse. He certainly knew how to pick winners. When he picked a big-race winner in the paper, everybody jumped on it, and Andy Beyer all of a sudden was ANDY BEYER.

Lou Hollis. Lou was a staff photographer who had an eye for a good shot. He also had an eye for the ladies – or, I should say, women had an eye for him. They would line up to have Lou shoot pictures of them in the darkroom. What happened in the darkroom stayed in the darkroom. Maybe it was the chemicals.

Fats. Fats wasn't a reporter exactly. Fats was a bookie who worked in the sports department. It might be more accurate to say that Fats worked the sports department.

A long, long time ago, before cell phones, before Blackberrys, before the Internet, there were just phones. Ordinary phones. Black phones with wires. And operators. That's how people at Point A talked to people at Point B. Oh, except for the teletype. That was a wired device that allowed words to be sent by wire from one place to another. I am telling you all of this because at racetracks there were no public phones. They did that to keep wise guys from past-posting the races, getting the finish right as it happened and beating out the bookies with the information to make the sure-thing bet. Watch the movie called The Sting and you will see how it worked.

Now, what better place for a bookie to be than in the sports department of a newspaper, where the race results were posted almost immediately by teletype, so he could keep from getting double-crossed by the sharpies at the track.

By the way, Fats wasn't fat at all. He was a small guy with a heart of gold. Short of cash before payday? Fats was good for fifty. Couldn't make it out for a burger? Fats would make it happen. He made himself indispensable. You could bet on it.

MOMENTS AT THE DAILY NEWS

Before I get into this, I have to talk about the Linotype machine.

Linotype machine

For the purpose of this story, it's important to understand the Linotype. It was like one of those little kids' toys where you drop a ball into a chute and it goes through a series of ramps and drops and curves and cracks and finally ends up at the finish.

The Linotype did this with words—and hot lead. The Linotype operator would type in words, and this magical machine in a hurdy-gurdy way would transform those words into strips of lead that the printer would then arrange into stories with everything justified right to left.

Each line would start in the same place.

Each line would end in the same place.

The lines in the story stacked like Legos.

The Linotype had a sense of finality about it. It was in lead. No eraser. No White-Out. Lead.

JFK'S ASSASSINATION

Everyone over the age of 60 remembers what they were doing that moment the day JFK was shot. I was a senior in high school. I had the day off. I was shooting baskets in the side yard. My mom opened the window and shouted out: "Kennedy's been shot!" I rushed inside and watched TV bulletin after bulletin coming out of Dallas.

John F. Kennedy made people my age pay attention to politics. He was a young, attractive Irish-Catholic who was loaded with energy and ideas that made a lot of sense. For me, it was no more American Bandstand. It was Kennedy's weekly press conference that became appointment viewing.

When JFK was shot and killed, I took it personally.

I couldn't stay home. I headed down to the Daily News. It, like other papers, put out a special edition on Kennedy and his assassination. I didn't witness this but was told that, to get the Daily News' special edition on the stands, Richard Hollander went down to the composing room and whispered words into the ear of a Linotype operator, who then struck those words into lead. Mr. Hollander's lips to lead. No room for error there.

Later that night I walked to the White House. It was only a few blocks from the newspaper. Lafayette Square was crowded with people standing and staring at the White House. It was eerie. It was sad. It made me feel older. But not in good way.

MATT KANE'S

I probably should have put Matt Kane in the reporter section because he was as much a part of the Daily News as anybody else. Matt owned Kane's Little Bit of

Ireland a bar located about 312 feet from the Daily News. It took several more steps on the way back.

Matt's Little Bit of Ireland had three stories. Matt called the first floor the newsroom. Regulars got brass nameplates screwed to their spot at the bar. I thought of the second floor as the Marine bar because it was popular with soldiers in the City. They would drink and fight; it wasn't uncommon to hear someone tumbling down the stairs. The third floor was the real bit of Ireland, a large room with a large bar and Irish singers and musicians.

Matt's was the first authentic Irish bar in Washington. On St. Patrick's Day Matt Kane's was the first and only stop to make. There was wall-to-wall people. The spilled beer on the floor was almost measurable. The music loud. All the men's rooms became ladies' rooms. Men were directed to a garage in the back. They would line up and pee into the gutter. Let's just say on St. Patrick's Day there was an Irish river running down the L Street alley.

For reporters at the Daily News, Matt Kane was family. Matt looked like a pug; he was a dark Irish man who was fond of a good round. Whether it involved alcohol or fisticuffs, Matt was at the ready. Matt would float you a loan, run a tab, give you advice—even if you didn't ask for it.

Big story day. Let's go to Matt's.

Somebody gets fired. Meet you at Matt's.

Hey, it's Wednesday. I'll be stopping off at Matt's.

So it was no big deal when one night after work, about five of us decided to go to Matt's for an adult beverage. No big deal—except on this night. The night city editor went along and brought all of the next day's stories with him to mark up. It seemed like a good plan until someone somehow spilled a pitcher of beer on the copy. The booth looked like a crime scene—soggy stories were stuck to the tables like some drunken decoupage experiment gone bad. This could have been disastrous because without these stories there would be no Daily News the next day. Heads would roll; careers would be crushed.

Then came the cook to the rescue. Over the greasy grill he used to fry burgers and bacon there was a wire with clothes pins that held the food orders so that each dish was prepared in a timely fashion. With surgical precision, Matt's cook peeled the stories off the table and clipped them, one-by-one, to the wire that held orders. In a short time, those beer drenched stories were "cooked" The paper might have been parchment crisp, but the stories were readable. With great care the city editor, cradling the copy like a newborn, carried the stories back to the Linotype operators and convinced them to make the copy newspaper ready. Nobody fired for that one. Time to celebrate at Matt's.

STOP THE PRESSES

August 25, 1967. Into the city desk at the Washington Daily News came a phone call from a tipster—the kind of call that makes a reporter's pulse race. The message: George Lincoln Rockwell had been shot at a shopping center in Arlington, Virginia. If true, that would be a big story, and if we moved fast we could still make the final edition.

George Lincoln Rockwell was known as the American Hitler. He was the leader of the American Nazi Party. He believed that blacks should be deported, and Jews should be sterilized. His followers and he had many goose-stepping protests around the city of Washington. From his headquarters in Arlington, Virginia, he broadcast his propaganda on a regular basis. He was like a bad virus. Just when you thought he was gone and forgotten he would stage another pop-up protest. This 49-year-old man caused more than his share of problems. And for someone who preached violence on a daily basis to be undone in a violent way, that's a story.

Lou Hollis and I raced from the newsroom and set a land speed record through the city to the Dominion Hills Shopping Center in Arlington. We were the first news people on the scene. There were some cops around, but we didn't hear any "Stay back! Stay back!" We were blood close to the crime scene. Lou Hollis snapped some pictures and sped back to the office to print the best picture and make the final, the photo so valuable the editors put a copyright on it.

Left by myself at the scene, I did my Daily Planet best to get the facts and get them fast. Once I realized what we had, I looked for a pay phone to call in the story. I saw one right inside one of the stores in the shopping center and hurried toward it. I was so excited that I failed to open the door and KABOOM! I hit the door and saw stars.

Not to worry. A head bump was not going to keep me from breaking the big one.

The story made it. The picture made it. And on that day the Washington Daily News, the little underdog tabloid on 13th Street, scooped the world. There is nothing quite like breaking a big story. I really don't remember how I returned to the Daily News that day, but it felt like I came back on a float. When I got to the newsroom there were handshakes, back pats, and countless attaboys. If there had been an MVP for reporting on that August day, I would have won it.

And then.

When the applause died down and my bosses and colleagues moved on to other things, a grizzled old news guy came up to me and, in gruff, whispered tones—well, the conversation went something like this.

Old news guy: "Collins, let me get this straight. You were the first reporter on the scene, right?"

Collins: "Yeah."

Old news guy: "And you were real close to the body?"

Collins: "Yeah."

Old news guy: "Then tell me this: HOW COME YOU DIDN'T GET HIS LAST WORDS?"

I think he was kidding. I hope he was kidding. He had to be kidding.

DANCING DECIMAL POINTS

There are statistics, and then there are police statistics.

American men are obsessed with keeping score. We are consumed by "the Count": the number of A's we got in school, the number of girls we dated, the number of times we've seen The Godfather, the number of cars we've owned, the number of beers we drank last night. And on and on and on.

Numbers have real-life consequences. The batting average or ERA of a baseball player can have a great impact on his salary. The number of votes cast for each candidate determines who wins elections. The number of viewers watching a television

Stories of cops and dancing decimal points

station's shows determines the station's rating. Being number one is important because being number two— well, no one really cares about number two.

So, it should be no surprise that the safety of a city is measured by the number of crimes committed in that city. And the great scorekeeper of crime has been and still is the FBI. It has categories and rules to chart crime in communities all around our country. For example, a grand larceny is described as a theft of more than $50. Anything below $50 is considered petty and, in most cases, not a reportable crime. One day I decided to go through the reports on the "petty crimes." What I found out was surprising.

Front Page Story:
Do District Police Falsify Reports To Trim Crime Rates?

My survey turned up evidence that hundreds of thefts of items valued at more than $50 were devalued by the cops and were, therefore, excluded from the monthly crime reports to the FBI. In the first six months of 1971, the DC police announced a decrease in thefts of items worth more than $50—from 5,381 in the first six months of 1970 to 3,804 in the first six months of 1971, a drop of about 29 percent. Not so fast.

We took a close look at some of those thefts and the values established by the DC police:

Stolen Pentax 35-millimeter camera valued at $20.

Stolen Vivatar 200-millimeter lens valued at $5.

Stolen audio-visual teaching machine and three American Tourister suitcases valued at $40.

Stolen adding machine and tape recorder valued at $49.

Well you get the idea. After our series of reports, the DC police let the victims establish the value of the items that were taken.

Front Page Story:
7 In 10 DC Slay Suspects Go Free

November 1971. At the time, the homicide rate in the District of Columbia was more than twice that of New York City. Murder was the most common cause of death for young men ages 15 to 44. We found that someone who committed murder in the city of Washington had a seven-in-ten chance of getting away with it. At the time, the City boasted of a 90-percent closure rate. We took a close look.

Only half of the suspects who were arrested were also indicted, and only a third of the suspects indicted were convicted. In the end, seven in ten may have gotten away with murder. It's the kind of thing that keeps you up at night.

KEY WITNESSES FEAR FOR LIVES IN TAILGATE MURDER CASE

This was a front-page story on July 4, 1971. Navy Commander William Rolland and his wife and children went to the fireworks display on the Washington Monument grounds. They were on their way home near Columbia Pike in Virginia when it happened. The Commander and his 19-year-old son shot and killed after a tailgating incident. The Rolland's Volkswagen was followed closely by a Grand Prix; the cars stopped;

words were exchanged. The Grand Prix driver pulled a gun and fired. Commander Rolland and his son were killed. Albert Spinner, the shooter's friend, was a key witness in the case. He was in a nearby car and gave me a blow-by-blow account of the double murder in an interview through a jailhouse window. He said that his friend had snapped and seemed to have enjoyed killing the Commander and his son. That interview turned out to be key evidence in the murder trial of the man who became known as the "Tailgate Killer."

THE FREEWAY PHANTOM

This front-page story was right out of the movies: Six young black girls were found dead along major highways leading out of the city. The evidence showed that they had been undressed and redressed by their killers after the murder. Some of the bodies had clothes on backwards or inside out. Some had no shoes. Four of the six had the middle name Denise. In one case investigators found a note: "Catch me if you can." The murders went on for months and then stopped after some gang members were arrested. They were picked up on some unrelated charges. But did they do it? For some, that's still an open question.

FRONT PAGE STORY: THE LAST SUPPER

This was one of the first big trials I covered. At one time, we reporters covering courts had a lot more freedom. We could park our cars right in front of the courthouse. We could walk into judges' chambers and talk face to face with them. Same with the prosecutors and with the U.S. Attorney himself. There was no spokesman or spokeswoman. The access was open and only a few people were afraid to talk. Very few.

Now, onto the case of the Last Supper.

In Washington in the 1970s, if you wanted a seafood dinner you headed to the southwest corner of the City. Near the water was a place called the Flagship. It sold the usual fare: steamed lobster, crab cakes, spiced shrimp, but the Flagship's specialty was not from the sea. It was from the oven: the buns – special, made-in-house rum buns brought to the table piping hot, drizzled with icing that covered the top and cascaded down the sides, forming a pond of deliciousness on the plate below. People liked the seafood. People loved the buns. The Flagship was a Washington favorite. It was a go-to restaurant for Robert and Linda Ammidown.

The Ammidowns were at the Flagship on October 1, 1971 – there for an early dinner. They had left their 11-year-old son, Bobby, with a babysitter at their Arlington home. After dinner, in the restaurant's parking lot, it got ugly. As Robert and Linda got into their car and started to drive off, a man jumped into the back seat. He said, "No one is going to get hurt – just do what I say." The man had a gun, and Ammidown did exactly what he was told to do. At the direction of the gunman. Ammidown drove across the East Capitol Street bridge and then down a dirt road close by the Anacostia River. From beneath the seat on the driver's side, the gunman pulled out a piece of clothesline and tied Robert Ammidown's hands behind his back. He had other plans for Linda. He led her to the edge of the water. He pulled her dress up over her head and raped her there in the dirt. Then he went back to the car and a short time later returned. A gun was in his hand. He looked at her. She looked at him. "Don't kill me," she pleaded. "I have an 11-year-old boy who means the world to me. Don't kill me."

The man placed the barrel of the gun behind Linda's right ear and shot her at point-blank range. Once. Then again.

The gunman ran off, got into a car with someone, and made his getaway. Ammidown loosened the ties around his hands. He drove down East Capitol Street past rows of homes. When he got to a gas station, he told the attendant, "My wife has been shot. Call the police."

The cops soon were all over the place near Linda's body by the river, all around Ammidown's car on that dirt road. They had few clues to work with. The piece of clothesline. A shell casing. There was evidence of a rape, but in 1971 DNA was just a concept taught in biology class.

Robert Ammidown was taken downtown to Homicide to be interviewed by detectives. Over and over he told the story of that murderous night. What he saw. What he heard. What he did. Over and over to a number of detectives.

One of those detectives was James Gainer. He sat with Ammidown for some time. "I felt sorry for him," Gainer said. "We both had kids about the same age. When I was talking to him I noticed he didn't cry, and when he gave the description of the suspect, he would use words like 'athletic,' 'well-built,' 'well-groomed'— almost like he was attracted to his wife's killer."

Gainer remembers feeling at the time that "there was something wrong with this case." And though detectives had suspicions, they had no evidence. In fact, they had nothing. But, when a wife is found murdered, the husband is almost always the first suspect. Turns out, Gainer's mother was a hostess at The Flagship; she had seated the Ammidowns that night.

Before marriage, Linda Ammidown was Linda Johnson. She was from a prominent family in Spotsylvania County, Virginia. That's where police took her son, and that's where police took Robert Ammidown after his lengthy interview at Homicide. Robert Ammidown was a retired Navy lieutenant commander who had a job at the Department of Commerce. According to investigators, Linda had the money and Linda had the power.

According to cops, it was something less than a torrid relationship. She wouldn't sleep with him until he did all his chores around the house. If he didn't spread the Spectracide on the lawn, there would be no sex. And if he did, she would go to the kitchen and get a shot of whiskey. Only then would the deed be done.

After an appropriate time, there was an appropriate funeral, and then Robert Ammidown felt he had to do something to get his son away from the city, to take his mind off his mother's death. So big Robert and little Bobby went off to the happiest place on earth: Disney World.

Back in the real world, the case was becoming a high-profile murder case with a capital M. The drumbeat was getting louder and louder; there was story after story about Linda Ammidown's horrific rape and murder after dinner at a popular restaurant.

Could diners ever feel safe again? Who was lurking in that parking lot?

The U.S. Attorney set up a task force. The marching orders: Solve this case. Try this case. Get the killer behind bars. Put the City at ease. In charge: Jim Sharp, a top-gun prosecutor.

While Ammidown and his son were at Disney World, someone called his office. He called every day between 11 a.m. and noon. He demanded to talk to Ammidown. He wouldn't leave his name. Ammidown's secretary thought this was odd—very odd. She called the cops. Two detectives went to Ammidown's office and waited for the call. The secretary put it through and a detective, Jack Moriarity, posed as Ammidown. The message from the voice on the other end went something like this: "I know you killed your wife. If you don't pay me, I go to the cops. Twenty-five thousand big ones."

Finally, the detectives had the break they needed. They set up a meet: Hot Shoppes, 14th Street. Moriarity sat alone at a table; Gainer was not far away. The outside was covered, too. Then came the wait. Then came a car with four men inside. One got out, a rough-looking man. They say his face looked like he'd been knocked down, gotten up, and then knocked down again. This guy had never met Ammidown, yet he knew that Ammidown most likely had something to do with the murder. Over the phone Moriarity had described himself, so when the extortionist got to the Hot Shoppes, he knew exactly where to sit. There was not much time for conversation. There wasn't even time for a glass of water. The detectives cuffed the guy and picked up the three other guys in the car. Then came a trip to Homicide and True Confessions. Now detectives were getting someplace.

The shakedown guy was Dutch Johnson, who had bragged that you could get anybody dead in Washington DC for $500. Tony Lee, a street hustler and a pool shark who was trying to raise money to open a bar, recruited Johnson to kill Linda Ammidown. Lee and Johnson had hatched a plan to kill her in a department-store parking lot in Arlington, Virginia but they scratched the plan because her son might be there. Finally, when it came to doing the deed, Dutch Johnson told Tony Lee, "No deal."

So, Lee decided to kill Linda Ammidown himself.

When Linda Ammidown turned up dead, Dutch Johnson knew that Lee likely had done it and that her husband was likely behind it. Johnson had never met Robert Ammidown, but he figured he could shake him down for some "quiet" money. He began calling Ammidown's office.

While at Disney World, Ammidown had no clue about Dutch Johnson's shake down plot or that Johnson had spoken with the cops. He had no idea how his life would change when he got back to Washington – that soon after he landed at the airport he would be cuffed, booked, and jailed.

The cops had Dutch Johnson. They had Robert Ammidown, but he wasn't talking. They needed Tony Lee. And Tony Lee was nowhere to be found.

How did Tony Lee get into the picture? A chance encounter brought him into it. Sometime earlier Ammidown and Lee had sat together on a flight. They talked and hit it off and continued to meet in Washington. Eventually, Lee asked Ammidown to partner with him to open a bar, but Ammidown refused, saying Linda wouldn't give him the money. Lee knew that Ammidown was not only unhappy at home but that he was also both meek and weak. He continued to bug Ammidown for money. Finally, when Ammidown said that Linda would never give him money to invest in a bar, Lee told Ammidown to get rid of her so they could get the money and get the bar up and running.

The police not only needed Lee, they needed evidence to link Ammidown and Lee to Linda's murder. They focused on the clothesline beneath the driver's seat of Ammidown's car, the clothesline that the gunman used to tie Robert Ammidown's hands. Where had that come from? Why was it under the driver's seat? Who put it there?

Detective Gainer wondered if Ammidown, himself, had acquired the clothesline and planted under his car seat. How could he prove it?

The detectives knew that Ammidown took a bus home each night. They went to his bus stop in Virginia and, lo and behold, what did they find there?   A hardware store.

They asked the store manager, "Do you remember selling that clothesline to this man?"

"Yes," he answered.

"Do you happen to have a receipt?"

"Yes."

"YES?"

"YES!"

The puzzle pieces were coming together. But the Tony Lee puzzle piece was still missing, and it was a big piece. The police needed to find Tony Lee. Lee had friends and relatives near New Orleans, so Detective Gainer went to New Orleans. He didn't find Tony Lee, but he did find a matchbook from Guys and Dolls, a Washington DC pool hall on Branch Avenue where Tony Lee hustled pool. After an extensive manhunt, the police arrested Lee in Washington and charged him with Linda Ammidown's murder. His plea: Not guilty. He said he had an alibi – that he was in a bar in southern Maryland when Linda was killed – that he wasn't even in the City.

Jim Sharp, the Assistant U.S. Attorney for the District of Columbia, was selected to prosecute Lee and Ammidown. Known to be tenacious, he was regularly assigned the most difficult and challenging cases as a senior trial lawyer in the Justice Department. To better understand Sharp you must understand how he got his job in the first place.

Jim Sharp received his J.D. from the University of Oklahoma. He wasn't in the top of his class. After law school he joined the Navy where he served with distinction as a trial lawyer in the JAG Corps in addition to acting as counsel to the Supreme Allied Commander when the nuclear submarine USS Scorpion was lost in the North Atlantic. After leaving the Navy, Sharp interviewed to become an Assistant U.S. Attorney with U.S. Attorney Dave Bress. He waited four hours for the interview. He knew he was an underdog – that most Assistant U.S. Attorneys graduated from the Ivies or Georgetown back then.

During the interview, Bress told Sharp, "I'm sure you're a pretty good lawyer, but . . . ." Sharp responded "I am, and if you don't hire me, I'm going to go out and become a defense lawyer, and every time I beat one of your Harvard boys in court, I'm going to come back to your office and remind you about it."

Sharp got the job. It was a good hire. It was a great hire. In a courtroom Sharp was a maestro. His preparations for the courtroom were meticulous. He was masterful at examining and cross-examining witnesses and at delivering compelling opening and closing speeches. He could read juries brilliaintly. And, he got guilty verdicts. He was part orator, part reverend. He was a natural. Now he had a big murder-for-hire case.

Jim Sharp needed help to destroy Tony Lee's southern Maryland bar alibi. He persuaded Ammidown to plead guilty and testify against Lee. Then he had Gainer drive from the murder scene to the alibi bar and clock it all the way. Gainer's tick-tock recreation of the night proved that Lee could have murdered Linda Ammidown and made it to southern Maryland to join his friends at the alibi bar.

At Lee's trial, Sharp went through the whole story with surgical precision. Lee's and Ammidown's meeting on the plane. Their meetings in Washington. Lee's dream of opening a bar. The Flagship. The clothesline beneath Ammidown's car seat. Ammidown's confession. Lee's tainted alibi.

The verdict: Guilty. Guilty of first-degree premeditated murder.

Sharp asked for the death penalty for Lee.

He told the judge that Tony Lee sentenced himself to death. "He knew if he killed Linda Ammidown, he could be sentenced to death. It was a planned and deliberate murder, and he forfeited his right to live amongst us."

Oh – and by the way – that judge was Judge John Sirica. He was known as "Maximum John." In court they would say, "If you go in front of Sirica, you might as well pack your over-life bag."

Judge Sirica sentenced Lee to death, but it turned into life. Ammidown got twenty-five years. And people began going back to The Flagship to get those rum buns.

NEWS BY THE NUMBERS

The Daily News was a "little engine that could" kind of paper. It was a blue-collar tabloid in a starched, button-down-shirt kind of town. It was a mid-morning tab sandwiched between the mighty Washington Post and the staid old Washington Star. The Daily News struggled for readers. It was a compact, easy read, made for subway riders except Washington didn't have a subway. Even though the paper was inexpensive, it never got its circulation up there with the big boys.

To compensate, the paper's back page featured a full page ad instead of sports news, like most tabloids. After all, money is money.

The Washington Post had Shirley Povich. The New York Times had James Reston. The Washington Daily News had ELMO.

ELMO looked like this:

365

147

098

Three columns of numbers across, three rows of numbers down, no two numbers the same.

To fully appreciate Elmo, you have to understand the importance of numbers and the numbers business. Long before the lottery and Powerball and Mega-millions, there was the numbers game. For many Washingtonians it was part of daily life. Get a cup of coffee. Eat breakfast. Feed the dog. Play the numbers.

Bets were made with bookmakers. In many neighborhoods, bookies were as common as the milkman, the postman, and even the corner cop.

The three-digit number was determined by the handle at a racetrack. Put fifty cents down, hit the number, get three-hundred bucks back. It was a chance for fast money, fun money, and it was home-delivered by the neighborhood numbers writer. If you were a little short, he would keep your number alive, no problem. He kept track of everything in his book.

The daily number wasn't published in the daily newspapers like the legal lotteries today. The numbers were often written on chalkboards at neighborhood liquor stores. It was a draw. Come in, check out the number, buy a bottle of booze. Everybody's a winner.

Now back to ELMO. Many readers thought ELMO forecast the daily number. Some would play the numbers across. Some would play the numbers down. Some did it diagonally. Every day someone in the sports department had to be ELMO. Many dark mornings in the newspaper's composing room. I WAS ELMO.

There were rules:

Never repeat the same numbers in the same order.

Never leave ELMO out of the paper.

And if someone called and asked to speak to ELMO, tell them he just left.

I was never a daily numbers player, but I must confess that every now and again I'd jump a number if one came my way.

Years ago, as a TV reporter, I was sent to Prince George County, Maryland, to cover the murder of a cabdriver. Driving a taxi around Washington can be a dangerous business. Cabbies are alone. They have cash. They are vulnerable.

In this case, someone hailed a cab, directed the driver to an apartment complex on Pennsylvania Avenue, put a gun to the cabbie's head, took his money, and shot him in his head. The driver tried to speed away but lost control of the cab and crashed into a fence and a stand of trees beside the road. It was a scary sight, the cab twisted in behind the trees. Ribbons of police tape strung from the cab to the apartment building and around the parking lot, and down the road. The place crawling with cops looking for clues and evidence of anything that might lead them to the killer.

I took my place right outside the police line, and as people came and went I asked them what they heard, what they saw, what they did, what they made of what happened. One of the people I talked to that morning was a well-dressed man. He wore a suit with a vest and he carried a pocket watch with a fob.. He walked from the apartment building with a purpose. I asked him if he knew what was going on. He didn't know anything about the murder. It was early in the morning and he was all dressed up; I just had to ask him where he was going.

With that he pulled out a key chain, and on it was a dog tag. "Son," he said, "my dog died about eleven years ago, and every day since I have played the number on his tag."

Collins: "What's the number?"

Well-dressed man: "8619. But it's never come up."

He said goodbye. I said goodbye. He went off to play the number. I went off to report the story about the robbery and murder of the cabdriver. It was live, and I was working out of a live truck. Sean Casey was my cameraman.

On the way back to the station we stopped for gas, but I really wouldn't call the place a gas station—it more like a lottery-playing center that occasionally sold fuel. Inside: a long cafeteria table surrounded by people drinking out of cans wrapped in brown paper bags. And on the table, all sorts of spent keno and lottery tickets. So while Casey was pumping gas, I went inside. The people at the table recognized me and said, "Hey, Pat Collins—what are you doing here?"

"Well," I said, "if you really want to know the truth, I'm here to play a number."

There was a gasp. You see, they knew about the cabdriver and they knew about the murder and one of them said, "Hey, you're not here to play that dead cabdriver's number, are you?"

Every cabdriver has a number, and for a minute they thought maybe I was going to try to profit from this poor man's death. I had to set them straight.

"No," I said. "I'm here to play a dead dog's tag number." Then I told them the story about the well-dressed man and the dog tag and the number 8619. Now, there is an unwritten code among numbers players: If you have a hot number, you should share it with others. On a Pick 4, it does not affect the jackpot.

At the window I made the bet: 8619, two dollars straight. Two-dollar box.

The bet down, the truck gassed, we left. It was a Friday night. We wanted to get our weekend underway. In a matter of minutes I had forgotten the whole transaction. Over the years I have made a number of spontaneous bets, stuffed the tickets in my pocket, and moved on with my life. After all, it's just chance – a gamble. You don't hold your breath for something like that.

Around nine o'clock that night the station started getting calls – frantic calls. "Where's Pat Collins? "How do we get in touch with Pat Collins? What's his phone number?"

The guys in the newsroom don't pass out numbers, and it wasn't until the next day that I realized what had happened. I picked up the paper, read the local stories, read the sports stories, scanned the national headlines, and—just for the heck of it—checked the number.

8619!

I couldn't believe it. I called my daughter and had her read the number just to be sure. It was a Saturday, and I had to go to a special claim center to get the money. It was well over ten-thousand dollars. They took about a third of it right there for taxes. I used the rest to pay off credit-card bills and make a mortgage payment. Within a couple hours it was all gone. I had nothing to show for it. No big TV. No car. No trip. Nothing.

My news manager at the time was a woman named Mary Ellen Donovan. Mary Ellen had a big heart and a double helping of emotions. You can imagine how she felt when later she lost her pet dog. So upset she was, well, she took the day off.

When she got it together and returned to work. And when the time was right and she was alone, I sidled up to Mary Ellen and expressed my deepest sympathy for her because of her deceased dog —and asked her if she happened to remember his tag number.

WATERGATE

June 17, 1972: the date of the infamous break-in at the Democratic National Committee Headquarters. I worked that story for weeks and weeks first at the Daily News with Scripps-Howard's Dan Thomasson and later at The Washington Star with Joe Volz. I posted stories about bugs going out, bugs going in, the burglars, and their possible accomplices. I had some singles and a few doubles, but no home runs. Nothing like the scoops developed by Bob Woodward and Carl

Bernstein at the Washington Post, especially after they hooked up with Deep Throat. Joe Volz and I were new to The Star after the story broke; we  were surprised that none of the big time reporters there wanted to get involved in it. The Star, closely aligned with the Republican Party, was an unlikely receptacle for a Watergate document dump.

Later Joe did a magazine piece entitled "None of the President's Men."

THE DEATH OF THE DAILY NEWS

July 12, 1972. I didn't see it coming. I don't think any of us saw it coming. I had a story in the paper that day about crime taking a dip. There were other stories about the Democratic convention in Miami and the Russians moving into a house on the Eastern Shore. But none of that really mattered. Not when Dick Hollander came out of his office – he rarely came out of his office – with his arms outstretched, his palms open to the sky. He made a Pope-like gesture motioning us all together. He didn't have to yell. We knew it was serious.

In a measured tone he told us that the next edition of the Daily News would be its last. That the Evening

Star had purchased certain assets of the Daily News and that we were finished.

It just wasn't fair. We were young and edgy. The Star, old and stodgy. It was like getting run over by a car driven by your grandmother. It just wasn't fair.

With no paper and no job, there was only one thing to do. Drink. For some reason, the wake ended up at the Collins' house on Capitol Hill. One by one, News people filed into our home and recounted all the big stories and good times, like old athletes retelling the stories of scores and accomplishments of past victories. And with each retelling of the stories the importance grew and grew.

Pulitzers for everyone. Alcohol has a way of doing that. When the booze ran out, there were hugs and kisses and handshakes and pledges to stay close and fight the good fight. Alcohol has a way of doing that.

The next day we would be sober and without jobs. The hunt would begin. Some would go to the Post. Some to the Star. Others out of the business altogether.

But we would never have as much fun as we all did at 1013 13th Street, Northwest

THE ARMY

In a Boonie hat back from Vietnam on a friendly beach

UNCLE SAM

Uncle Sam lies. I know it now. But I wish someone had told me that way back when it mattered. I went to a military high school; there were uniforms, parades, inspections, rifles. In my first year at the University of Notre Dame, I had a choice: take physical education or join ROTC. Since I went through four years of army training in high school, I would be exempt from training my freshman year of college if I joined ROTC. Let me go back over that again: Take phys-ed and spend a couple of days a week running laps and doing jumping jacks or join ROTC and have to do nothing for the first year.

Oh – one other thing. Did I mention that the war in Vietnam was going full blast, and that some people were getting drafted right out of school? Surely the war would be over by the time I graduated. I knew that. Everybody knew that. Didn't they?

That first year of not doing anything went extremely well. The second year was okay; the third year, fine. The fourth year, not so good. You see, that war in Southeast Asia was still fired up, and for me and other soon-to-be lieutenants in Uncle Sam's Army, it was decision time.

We had to pick three branches of the army, one of them had to involve combat. The first two choices pretty easy.

Choice Number 1: Adjutant General Corps—an administrative branch that did a lot of paper-pushing. It had its own motto:" Twinkle, twinkle, little shield, keep me off the battlefield."

Choice Number 2: Supply—an almost guaranteed rear assignment dealing with uniforms, arms, vehicles. It would be the army's version of Walmart.

Then came the combat pick. I chose Artillery. It would put me in a war zone, but the big guns would be way back from the front. Certainly, it would give me a safe place if I had to go—which, by the way, I really didn't want to do.

Those were my three picks. It was like a real-life army game of "rock, paper, scissors."

What did I get? MSC.

MSC? I had to ask somebody what it meant. MSC means Medical Service Corps. You see, Uncle Sam, with all of his great wisdom, decided to put this English major in the Medical Service Corps.

Not to worry, my fellow soldiers said—it's better than the infantry.

There was one more play here. You see, because I was in ROTC, I could delay my entry into the service for one year. Surely the war would be over by then. So I took the 365-day decision plan. And, of course, the war continued warring right along.

INTO THE ARMY

Then came 1969 and Orders to report to Ft. Sam Houston, Texas. There I began training to become a medic. I gave practice shots to oranges and grapefruit, trying not to stab myself with the needle. I learned how to check an airway, stop bleeding, and keep the wounded alive until a real doctor could practice some real medicine. This went on for a couple months, and then – and then, and then – oh my God, word from Washington.

When you are in the army and you hear word from Washington, your ears perk up. At least mine did when I heard that there was a search on for a general's aide. Every general has an aide. He stands next to him in receiving lines, handles correspondence and details of the day. The Medical Service Corps has one general and only one aide – and that general is stationed in Washington. My hometown. If I got that job I could go home, work part-time for a newspaper, and do my entire tour standing on my head.

I was inspired. I got a high and tight haircut, shaved my mustache, and wrote the best damn résumé, slaving over every word. They had to pick me. It's my town. I did everything but get on my knees. But maybe that's what I should have done. Because it turns out that a general's aide can't be taller than the general, and they told me I was about two inches too tall.

Really? Well, that's the excuse they gave me anyhow.

Back to the oranges and grapefruit and needles and olive-drab army life.

I was ordered to become a company commander at the Medical Training Center in Ft. Sam Houston. Hooray. It was not exactly a prime assignment, but it was not Vietnam, and my soldier buddies said it would probably keep me stateside for my whole two-year obligation.

There I was, company commander of about 700 trainees learning to become medics. They were from all over the country, all walks of life, and for several months I would act as their father, mother, counselor. Sometimes I had no idea how many soldiers I had, what they were doing, or where they were. Of course, from time to time the MPs would help sort things out. And let's not forget—I wasn't in Vietnam.

One of my duties was to reply to Congressional Inquiries. If you are in the Army and want to put some heat on your commander, just drop a note to your

Congressman, tell him things aren't going well, and that you're disillusioned and depressed. Ask him to look into it. In a very short time, your commander will receive a Congressional Inquiry.

A number of soldiers in my company were lawyers, and, boy, could they write letters to their Congressmen. "Food's too cold." "Not enough sleep." "Had to march too much." Upon receiving such a plaintiff missive from a constituent, the Congressman would fire off a Congressional Inquiry. I quickly learned that each Congressional Inquiry must be answered in about 48 hours. Everything must grind to a halt until a reply was sent to the Congressman. A customary reply went something like this: "Dear Congressman [Fill-in-the-blank]: We, too, are concerned about Johnny's complaints and will do what we can to make his stay here at Ft. Sam more comfortable."

This may be more than you want to know about being a commander in a training company, but it's something that has always stuck in my mind because there are always some people out there who try every little thing to get out of doing what they are supposed to do. And it's just not fair. If I am too detailed, skip over the next couple of paragraphs and move on with the story.

For those of you who stayed with me, let me explain emergency leave. At my discretion a soldier could be allowed to return home to address family situations that required his attention. If a soldier missed ten days of training, he was required to be recycled into another company to resume his course work.

Conversations between a CO and a soldier went like this:

CO: "Johnny, things all right at home?

Johnny: "Yeah, my mother has a bit of a cold."

CO: "Well, you know those colds can be tricky. Will she be all right?

Johnny: "I think so."

CO: "Maybe you should go home and see her."

Johnny: "Can I?"

CO: "Sure. Why don't you take some emergency leave?"

Problem solved. Troublemaker transferred.

Uncle Sam lies. Okay, not always and maybe not big, bold, notorious lies, but Uncle Sam certainly doesn't always tell the whole truth, either. Remember "Pat, if you become a company commander, there is little chance you will ever get orders to go to Vietnam"? Little chance? Well don't bet on it. After I had been a commander for less than a year, I received the order: Lt. Collins you are going to Nam.

My experience in Vietnam has stayed with me like an emotional and psychological tattoo. I remember flying off to war in a Braniff airplane. In those days, Braniff planes were painted in bright, Crayola colors. My plane was orange. I was convinced that when I landed someone was going to shoot me right then and there—dead as soon as I got off the plane.

4 Patrick J. Collins
1st Sqd Hdqt Medics
11th ACR, APO 96257

Free

VIA AIR MAIL

Dr & Mrs T. F. Collins
2600 Queens Chapel Road
Hyattsville, Maryland 20782

FROM MY LETTERS HOME:
WELCOME TO VIETNAM

Soldiers in Viet Nam were afforded
free franking privileges, but we had to write our
letters on onion skin paper to minimize the postal
weight and worry. I asked my parents to hold on to my
letters - just in case. I found some of them in a cigar
box. They reminded me of what I was thinking and
feeling in Vietnam.

I landed at Bien Hua airport 5 Feb 70 or was it 4
Feb 70? At the time it mattered little. I had been on the
plane for some 23 hours with a short layover in Luzon
in the Philippines. My body as well as my mind felt as if
it traveled 1,500 years back in a time machine. Before
landing the stewardess announced that she and the
crew were proud of their fighting men who came to
Viet Nam to risk their lives for their country. I almost
vomited. She would fly away, and I had to spend a year
in this dump.

When I walked off the plane, the terminal looked like any other airport terminal. There were TVs, snack bars, people just walking around. The only thing different: Everyone was wearing the same uniform.

On the plane were 17 Medical Service Corps officers. Of those, 14 MSC's were assigned to hospitals—hospitals with air-conditioning, warm food, and female nurses. Only three MSC's ended up in combat units. I was one of them. As it turns out, one of my friends at Ft. Sam saw my name on a levy. He was with the 11th ACR, and he requested that I be assigned there. This is the way it went.

Assigning officer: "Smith, 24 Evac hospital. Evans, 3rd field hospital. Rogers, 93rd Evac hospital. Collins, 11th ACR."

Collins: "What kind of hospital is the 11th ACR?"

Assigning officer: "That's no hospital that's the 11th Armored Cavalry Regiment."

I think I need a priest.

Fear. One of the biggest lessons I learned: You can only be frightened to death for so long. For the first month I was ever so careful. I always wore a flak vest and tried to sleep in a safe place. During a rocket or mortar attacks I would always take cover. But I could only be scared for so long. After a while I became fatalistic. If the bullet had my name on it, I'd be done. It didn't mean I became reckless; it just meant that, after a while, I stopped getting scared.

LIFE IN THE FIELD

Taking a shower: Every day everyone got five gallons of water in a big green can. We left the cans in the sun to warm up. In the evening, I poured the water into canvas shower bag stood on a wooden pallet, hoisted the bag over my head,released the water, sudsed up, and rinsed off – and just about then a helicopter would buzz by, creating a dust storm that coated my body with dirt.

Camp followers: No mattered where we ended up, outside our perimeter locals would set up their version of a shopping center. For sale: fake Rolex watches; mirrors; all sorts of items made from old Coke cans; pot; and sex. VD was no small problem in Vietnam.

The Cambodian Incursion and the search for COM Z. Intelligence had determined that a major supply line for the Viet Cong came from a military fortress known as the COM Z in Cambodia. We were dispatched to find it. It was supposed to be a big secret. The commanders said to prepare for a big conflict, order lots of bandages, drugs, medical supplies and start stockpiling. Then one day, without warning, we pulled up stakes and off we went to Cambodia. A couple things I remember: a little wooden sign alongside the dirt road that said, "Welcome to Cambodia." I thought that was a very kind gesture. And then I learned our super-secret mission was in the papers back home days before our surprise move. Our country has always had a hard time with secrets.

FROM MY LETTERS HOME:
CAMBODIA

We were in Cambodia from 9 May 70 until 25 June 70. The first period went quietly, the only excitement being a few medical missions in Cambodian villages. We were used as decoys, performing perfunctory exams and care while intelligence boys examined the villages for suspicious activity. There were some anxious moments but nothing came of them.

The trouble came in the last 15 days when our helicopters took ground-to-air fire three and four times a day and our troops were ambushed in the mountains and mortared at night. Our casualty rate soared; in one 24-hour period one troop lost five men. In the days to follow, another troop lost so many men it had to combine two platoons into one.

Getting Out. On the 25th of June we left. It was no surprise. In fact, as I recall, Washington announced our departure date a week before we made the move. We are just not good at surprises. The thought was that the North Vietnamese would attack us and make it look like they were driving us out of Cambodia. So the night before, we moved our base camp. Everything that wouldn't start didn't go. Then they called in a B-52 strike on our old location just in case the enemy was out doing some treasure hunting. We were close by the bombing—it sounded like a thousand ambulances screaming out of the sky. The ground trembled. I spent the night sleeping under a tank. Where is that priest?

THE MALARIA WAR

Aside from getting shot, one of the big fears in Vietnam was malaria. Daily and weekly we would take anti-malaria pills, which would bring about rampant cases of diarrhea and long lines at portable toilets. It was serious stuff. There were 34 cases of malaria in our squadron in less than one month. I was spared – fortunately.

NEAR DEATH ENCOUNTERS

I was flying in a helicopter when a sniper opened fire and, brrraap, four bullet holes right through the floor. It was a Hail Mary moment. Note: When flying in a helicopter during a war, always sit on your flak vest. You never want to have to explain how you got shot in the ass.

I was driving an open-air ambulance (a jeep with a rack for a stretcher) on a dirt road when all of a sudden - sniper fire. No surprise, but this time I was alone. I floored it. Dirt danced all around me, but no blood was shed.

I was at a bordello in DiAn when gangsters robbed the place. It was like the wild, wild West. Shots flew every which way. I jumped out a second-floor window. It was a moving experience – just not the one for which I had hoped.

R&R

Rest and Recuperation. Everybody in-country got at least one week out of country. I chose a week in Hong

Kong. I was close to our helicopter pilots and took R&R with them. In many ways we partied like there was no tomorrow. When we landed, some official gave us a list of the off-limits places in Hong Kong, which, of course, became the directory for all the spots we hit.

Merchants lured us into clothing stores, seated us in large, throne-like chairs, brought us wine and booze, and then sold us custom suits – silk suits. They seemed like a good idea at the time, but when we put them on it was like Frank Sinatra and the Rat Pack. Mama sans waved us into their bars and tried to get us 'dates' with the models they showcased like Rockettes on the dance floor. Those girls loved GIs—for a price. At restaurants there were GI specials. On the street, there were rickshaw races. There was no time to sleep, no time to waste. There was no time.

THE GRIM FACTS OF WAR

Someone once described war as long periods of boredom followed by moments of sheer terror. He was right. Much of our time was spent getting ready for contact. We were a tank unit. We had guns – really big guns. The Viet Cong were reluctant to engage us head-on. We had to seek them out. We were vulnerable to mines and rockets and ambushes. They took their toll.

Sadly, some of our casualties were from friendly fire. Those big guns sometimes were not pointed in the right direction.

One of the enemy's most effective weapons was something called a rocket-propelled grenade. It was armor-piercing. It would slice through the walls of a tank and explode like a grenade. We never dangled our legs inside a tank—an RPG could cause instant amputation. So we would sit Indian style on top of the tanks. But if our big guns were not pointed the right way, our troopers became sitting ducks.

It was in Vietnam that I came face-to-face with death. It was in Vietnam that I realized how precious life can be. I could not afford to dwell on it at the time. It would make me too cautious. It would make me crazy.

The medics with whom I served were well trained. They knew how to treat sucking chest wounds, start IVs, clear airways, stop bleeding, administer morphine, and call for a Med Evac helicopter. Because most of our wounded were in hot landing zones where more gunfire was expected, we used our own helicopters to evacuate our wounded.

Our choppers had gunners and daring pilots— they never refused a call for help, and I never hesitated to call them. In fact, today I still remember my Vietnam call sign: Basket 4-4. We had a mobile medical hospital attached to us with some skilled surgeons at the ready. Still, there were times the wounds were too severe, when nothing more could be done. I remember putting troopers in body bags, tagging the bags, and sending them back to the rear.

SHORT-TIMER: GOING HOME

As it got closer and closer to my departure date, I got more and more careful. Just about everybody in Vietnam had a short-timer's calendar marking off each day, one by one by one. With each short-timer's mark came acts of newbie caution – a helmet and a flak vest always within reach, a weapon always close by. I was issued a .45 caliber pistol, but I chose to carry a grenade launcher. It looks like a cartoon gun. It may look funny, but it can neutralize anyone who gets too close.

At night I was careful to sleep under cover. I'm not talking blankets here, I'm talking bullet-proof cover. Nobody wanted to buy it with just a few days left in country. So when my departure date got close, real close, I huddled with other short-timers in the rear until we flew away.

I returned from Vietnam to an Army base in California. First, I got paid in cash, a lot of cash – more than I could carry. Then I checked into a room, took some time using a flush toilet, had a warm shower and a lobster dinner, and boarded a flight home. The plane landed in Baltimore. There was no brass band; there were no banners. I was told to "Stand over there, soldier—we'll get to you in a minute." At the terminal gate, there were just my parents and my nephew. I tossed him my cap and said, "Hold on to this—you may need it someday." He smiled. I smiled. And that was it. I was home and safe, and that was good enough for me.

THOUGHTS ABOUT VIETNAM

Many of the soldiers in Vietnam thought the war was a waste, that we were being manipulated by politicians far away, that a lot of young men lost their lives for nothing. We used to joke that we were there to save the Coca Cola Company. It didn't matter. We were there. We did what we had to do to get home in one piece. I was close to the men with whom I served. We all vowed to get together when we came home, but we never did.

I want to make it clear that what I did was nothing compared to the Rangers, the infantry men, and the Marines who, on a daily basis, performed heroic acts to save the lives of their fellow soldiers and advance our cause in that crazy war.

The Coca Cola Company should be proud.

Though our involvement in Viet Nam was a mistake, I don't regret the time I spent in the military. I still draw on the things I learned and experienced in the Army. Our military is a merit-based mission-focused organization. Over the years it has done a lot to bring our country together. In the service people of all colors, all religions, all political persuasions, country boys and city slickers must all learn to work together to get the job done. And most of the time, when they get out that kind of understanding carries over to civilian life.

4

BACK TO REPORTING

THREE

> The Holy Trinity
> Three Wise Men
> Three of a kind
> Three Musketeers
> Three Blind Mice
> All Gaul is divided into three parts

In religion, in literature, in the way we live our lives, the number three seems to have a mystical and significant meaning. Sometimes good, sometimes evil. If you're Irish, ask your grandmother; she will tell you, sometimes bad things come in threes.

PART 1

In the third month of America's bicentennial year, in the city of Washington, vicious, violent acts were carried out by three men with surnames associated with kindness: Bishop, Goode, and Angell.

Bradford Bishop

On March 1, 1976, Bradford Bishop killed his entire family—his mother, his wife, and his three children. The crime scene: their California-style home in the Carderock community close by the city of Washington.

Bishop had quite a resume. He was a Yale graduate, had degrees from UCLA, Middlebury College, and the University of Florence. He spoke five languages: English, Spanish, French, Serbo-Croatian, and Italian. He had served abroad in Italy and Africa.

At the time of the crime, Bishop was a State Department employee assigned to the State Department's headquarters. His title: Assistant Chief of Special Activities. He had counterintelligence training from the Army.

Bishop was 39 years old and was said to be a man of great ambition, but on the first of March 1976, he received word that he was not going to be promoted. He told his secretary that he felt ill. He left work early and began his mission of death.

At a store not far from his home, Bishop bought a hammer and a gas can and stopped for gas. Then, with a great sense of purpose, he drove to the murder scene, his own home.

The order of death:

His 37-year-old wife, Annette, whom he beat with the hammer.

Then his mother, after she returned home from walking the family's golden retriever.

And finally his three sons, one by one, ages fourteen and ten and five.

The only life spared: the family dog, Leo.

He loaded all five bodies into the back of the family station wagon, and with Leo as his companion, Bishop drove to some parkland in North Carolina 300 miles away.

On March 2, a forest ranger in North Carolina spotted smoke drifting out of a wooded area. When he investigated, he discovered a mound of bodies on fire, stacked like logs in a shallow grave. At the time, it was just a horrific, mysterious find in North Carolina. The discovery didn't take on its full meaning until eight days later.

On March 10, Bishop's Carderock neighbors started to get suspicious. There had been no sign of Annette or Bradford Bishop or the mother or of the kids. No one had seen Leo the dog. They called 9-1-1.

On police scanners we heard about the activity in Carderock and off I went to the scene. I almost always start at the scene. The scene is the centerpiece of most crime stories. You can learn a lot by watching the cops gather evidence, by talking to investigators as they come and go, and by talking to neighbors.

At that scene on that day in that modern style house nestled in the woods I didn't have to ask many questions to figure out that something terribly wrong had happened inside that house. Cops found blood on the front steps. Inside there was blood on the floors, on the ceilings, and in some places trails of blood from wall to wall—the signs and smell of death all around.

But there were no bodies. There was no sign of the Bishop family. The neighbors were upset. This was not the kind of place you expect to find this kind of violence. It took days before it all came together, and even then the case never closed.

On March 18, the Bishop family station wagon was found abandoned in the Great Smokey Mountains, about 400 miles away. Inside: a bloody blanket and some dog biscuits.

Bradford Bishop was nowhere to be found. In fact, Bradford Bishop has never been found. There have been sightings of him in Germany, in Switzerland, in Spain, and in many other places. But no sighting was ever confirmed. His diplomatic passport, his fluency in so many languages, his counterintelligence training all gave him an edge on the lawmen trying to hunt him down.

So why did he do it?

It was reported that his wife and his mother often ridiculed him about his job performance and his inability to advance. Some believe this savage act of murder was his way of getting even—and getting off to a fresh start.

Arthur Frederick Goode

I have to start in the middle of this story because something happened in this case that I have never seen before or since in a court of law. I was there in that Fairfax County, Virginia, courtroom when it all went down.

Arthur Frederick Goode had been convicted of murdering a little boy who lived in the County. The judge gave him an opportunity to make a statement before sentencing.

Goode stood, looked directly at the judge, and said: "Judge, you may as well sentence me to death, because if I get out and run across another little boy— another sexy little boy – he will never make it home again."

Then Ian Rodway, Goode's defense attorney, made a statement of his own. "Your honor, under the circumstances, I think the maximum sentence is appropriate in this case."

I have sat through a lot of trials, but until Goode's, I had never seen a defense attorney ask a judge to throw the book at his client. When you understand what Goode did, you might understand why.

March 20, 1976: In a wooded area near Tyson's Corner, Virginia, Arthur Frederick Goode forced 11-year-old Kenny Dawson to undress, sexually assaulted the 65-pound boy, and then strangled him. He did this in front of 10-year-old Billy Arches, a boy he had kidnapped earlier in Baltimore, but he didn't kill Billie.

Arthur Frederick Goode was a longtime self-confessed pedophile. In an interview he said what he really wanted to do was find a way to legally marry a young boy.

Goode was originally from Hyattsville, Maryland. As a teenager he had been arrested a number of times for indecent exposure and assaults on little boys. Each time his parents bailed him out. Each time he was released in their custody. Each time he went back and did it again.

In Dundalk, Maryland, he took a 13-year-old into the woods, had sex with him, and kept all his clothes.

Later, a passerby saw the boy wandering out of the woods naked.

In an interview with movie producer John Waters, Goode said: "The only thing I do is fellatio – you know, oral sex. That's the main thing—hugging and kissing. But I don't do that sodomy. I don't like that either way."

Arthur Frederick Goode just couldn't stay away from little boys. In March 1975, he assaulted a nine-year-old boy while out on bail after being arrested for sexually assaulting an 11-year-old boy.

He stayed out of jail by voluntarily committing himself to the Spring Grove Mental Hospital, a minimum-security facility outside Baltimore. In a matter of weeks, he simply walked out of the hospital. In an interview he explained, "They locked me up on a locked ward. When I escaped, I had a master key."

After his escape, Goode went to his parents' home in St. James City, Florida. There he continued to hunt down little boys.

March 5, 1976: Goode persuaded a nine-year-old boy to help him "try and find something" in the woods. "I told the boy he was going to die," Goode said. "I told him how I was going to kill him. I asked him if he any last words, and he said, 'I love you, ' and then I strangled him."

Goode was questioned by Florida police in that case but was not arrested. He took the bus back to Baltimore, where he kidnapped Billy Arches, the ten-year-old son of a professor. He took Billy to Washington, where they went sightseeing for a few days. On March 20, 1976, Goode kidnapped Kenny

Dawson, took him into the Tysons Corner woods, and strangled him while Billy stood and watched.

A few days later Goode was arrested in Fairfax, Virginia. Eventually, he was tried and convicted of murdering Kenney Dawson. It was after that conviction that he asked to be executed. At the time there was no death penalty in Virginia. But in Florida, Goode's wish came true. There he was tried for the murder of the nine-year-old he strangled on March 5, 1976; Arthur Frederick Goode was put to death on April 5, 1984.

His final meal: steak, corn, broccoli, and cookies.

His final request: permission to spend time with a sexy little boy.

Robert Angell

March 26, 1976: That morning I was at the Spring Grove Mental Hospital working on a follow-up story about Arthur Frederick Goode and how he'd just walked away from the place. I didn't get far on Goode's story that day because, as my cameraman, Bruce Buckholtz, and I pulled onto the hospital grounds, we heard a call on the police radio: two cops had been shot behind the Montgomery Mall in Bethesda, Maryland.

Being in a big, live-camera truck did not slow Bruce down. NASCAR-quick, he zigged and zagged through traffic on various highways. Once on the scene, Bruce began a live shot and I moved around trying to figure out what had happened. I could tell it was serious: the place was crawling with cops; people were being questioned; cars were being searched. Bruce is lightning fast with the microwave, the mast on that truck is about 65 feet long; it is powered up with compressed air; and sometimes it seems like it takes forever for it to fully extend. That day we needed the whole stick to send our feed to the station. We needed to get the mast up and on air as soon as possible. Two Montgomery County police officers had been shot and were on the edge of death. A manhunt was under way.

Earlier that morning, a young man wearing a ski mask and carrying a shotgun had walked into a bank and demanded money. When he got what he wanted, he casually walked out to a red Chevy car and drove off. It was something less than a perfect crime. During the robbery, one of the employees tripped the alarm and, as the getaway car pulled away, someone wrote down the car's tag number.

Word of the robbery was broadcast quickly on the Montgomery County police channel. Police Corporal John Frontczak spotted the suspect in the car near Montgomery Mall and gave chase. The red Chevy raced behind the mall and into an area that kids used as a lover's lane.

On his radio Captain James Daly heard about the chase and headed to the field to help make the arrest in his unmarked car. What happened after that was a moment from hell.

The bank robber slipped out of the red Chevy and, as Daly and another officer arrived on the scene, he shot each officer in the head.

Officer Steve King was there moments after the shooting. He recalls it this way:

"Two officers with a ton of experience, and they had been ambushed. What chance did I have? I knew right then I was going to get shot. I was low, crawling through the grass while looking up at the trees, trying to spot the suspect before he spotted me. I was able to get back to my cruiser to call for help. This in and of itself was frustrating because it seemed like every cruiser was trying to get on the air to tell other units where to look for us. I then returned to John and Captain Daly to tend to their wounds while waiting for what seemed like an eternity for anyone else to arrive."

The search for the suspect was delayed for some time as emergency crews rushed to the scene to aid the fallen officers.

Police had the getaway car. The red Chevy had been stolen from the Mall. In it the police found a 20-gauge shotgun and a twenty-dollar bill stolen from the bank.

But on that day, there was no arrest. The killer got away.

Two days later there came a big break in the case: A man by the name of James Angell walked into a police station and told the cop on duty he thought his son Robert was the man who robbed the bank and killed the cops.

Robert Daly Angell was 19 years old, a tenth-grade dropout listed as AWOL from the Army. Hours after his father tipped off the police, Angell was arrested in South Carolina. He pleaded guilty to the murder of the two officers and was sentenced to life in prison.

It's just a coincidence that Robert Daly Angell lived in the Carderock Springs community, close to Bradford Bishop's home

PART 2

For some reason—I don't know why—people who do really bad things often have three names. Names that are hard to forget. The names of their victims fade quickly, but the names of the killers and the details of their villainous acts stick like an indelible stain in the annals of crime.

Billie Austin Bryant

This is the story of Billie Austin Bryant. Born in Mount Olive, North Carolina, in 1940, Bryant grew up in a gray farmhouse near some tobacco farms. He moved to Baltimore with his mother and learned to be an automobile mechanic. In 1964 he settled in Southeast Washington with his wife and two children. Bryant and a friend opened an auto-repair shop. Neighbors described him as an" average, hard-working guy." Until 1967. That's when Billie's life went south. He got into a fight with his business partner, lost his money, and ended up broke.

Billie Austin Bryant was desperate.

January 1967: A lone bandit wearing a black knit shirt robbed the DC Capital Savings & Loan. The takeaway: $1,300 dollars.

April 7, same year. Same guy, same description, stole $1,272 dollars from Jefferson Savings & Loan. A few days later there was another robbery at another bank; this time the take about $2,600.

Billie Austin Bryant was on robbery roll. The cops wanted him badly. Acting on a tip, they tracked Billie down to a Northeast DC motel where he had checked in under the name Freeman Morris and was living with a young woman.

Police barged in the door. Billie reached for a derringer, but he didn't pull the trigger of the tiny gun. When questioned, he said, "If it wasn't for this young lady, I would have shot the first four cops who came in, and you'd have never taken me alive." These words foreshadowed the deadly deed yet to come.

Billie Austin Bryant was found guilty of those bank robberies and sentenced to 18 to 54 years in jail. The judge in the case was the now famous Maximum John Sirica.

Off to jail went Billie Austin Bryant, but he wasn't there for long. Three months later after entering the Lorton Correctional Facility, he drove a car through its gates and was on the loose. In 1969 he re-surfaced, driving a maroon Cadillac. Not long after that he was back to his old ways. He robbed $4,000 from the branch of a bank where he kept his own money. A teller recognized him, called 9-1-1, and another manhunt began.

After Billie's escape from Lorton, cops and agents routinely checked out his estranged wife's apartment on Yuma Street, Southeast. Guys on the run always seem to return home. It's a magnet. Maybe it's the cooking. Cops know that, so they always keep an eye on home base.

One January day in 1969, the cops found two FBI agents shot to death, one body on top of the other. The scene Apartment 12 on the third floor of 133 Yuma Street. It was rare for two FBI agents to be killed at the same place on the same day. Agent Edward Woodriff, 27, had been shot in the head. He was the first black FBI agent killed in the line of duty. Agent Anthony Palmisano, 26, had been shot in the chest.

Billie Austin Bryant was long gone. He had climbed down a tree in the back and vanished. The Agency was not happy. The cops were not happy. The City was not happy.

Billie's disappearance led to a massive manhunt, like something out of a mob movie. FBI agents—scores of them in long coats and with long guns—descended on the neighborhood, searching apartment after apartment. In this door; up these stairs; in that door; down those stairs. They were everywhere. The cops were there, too, some taking positions on rooftops with guns drawn just in case Billie were to peek out into the open.

The FBI and police did spot-checks of cars on the street. They went through a wooded area; they went up and down a nearby creek bed. It went on for hours and hours until they got the tip they needed. It came from a dog—not a police canine but a white Huskie named Chico.

Robert Ross lived in an apartment at 167 Mississippi Avenue, Southeast, in a building close by the murder scene. Robert Ross had the flu and had stayed home from work that day. He noticed all the police activity in the neighborhood and heard news bulletins on TV about the murder of the agents. More important, though, he was concerned about the strange behavior of his dog, Chico. You see, Chico kept barking and whining and pawing at the apartment door.

Mr. Ross tried to ignore Chico, but Chico would not be ignored. Ross opened the apartment door and heard scratching sounds near a trap door to the attic in the hallway. Mr. Ross slipped back inside and, in a quiet voice in a room away from the door, called police.

In a flash the cops showed up. One pointed a shotgun at the trap door.

"Anybody up there?" a cop yelled.

"Yes, I'm up here," said a voice from the attic. "I'm Billie Austin Bryant."

Billie dropped his gun through the attic opening, eased his burly body down through attic's trap door, and was taken away without a fight.

His mother had said, "Billie always had a love for guns and cars, but he always respected them."

Billie Austin Bryant is a name long remembered in the history of Washington crime. The names of the fallen agents, not so much.

It's the twisted way of the world.

Benny Lee Lawson

Go to DC police. Go to DC police headquarters now. That was the call I got from my boss on that day. At the time I was working a story in Maryland, but when I heard those words in that tone, I knew I was in for a big change and a big story.

I rushed to the scene. When I arrived, I thought I was back in a war zone. Helicopters flew in to evacuate the wounded; workers fled from the building to protected areas; SWAT teams in tactical gear rushed in through all doors.

I saw police officers crying.

There had been a homicide inside the Homicide squad. Not just a single death, but the calculated slaughter of three law-enforcement officers—two FBI agents and a police detective sergeant. All at the hands of one man: Benny Lee Lawson. But Benny's target, the man he wanted to kill, was not there.

1994 was a bumper year for the street drug business in the city of Washington. As the competition for territory increased, so did the street violence. In upper Northwest Washington, the First and Kennedy Street Crew controlled the action. When they felt betrayed, double-crossed, or threatened, they let their guns do the talking.

Such was the case on November 13, 1994, when five people were shot in a row house, including an 87-year-old man. Three of the victims died. Police put on a full-court press to find the killers. The First and Kennedy crew members were the prime suspects.

Benny Lee Lawson was at the top of the list. Lawson, a 25-year-old street thug, had been in an out of trouble most of his adult life. Detectives leaned on him. They seized his car, which made Benny unhappy. Then they took him "downtown" to police headquarters, which made him even more unhappy. Nobody liked to be taken "downtown" because that meant the cops could get you alone, and there was no telling what they might do or what you might say. For a suspect in a big murder case, nothing good could happen "downtown." But Benny was "downtown" in the homicide squad room where he met Detective Lou Hennessey's detective gave Benny some news that made him even more unhappy: DNA evidence from Benny's car linked him to the triple homicide on Kennedy Street.

Benny was worried. He wasn't the only one. So was Kobi Mowatt, the leader of the Kennedy Street Crew. Word on the street was that Benny might be cooperating—that Benny might be a snitch. None of this was good news for Benny. So he decided to gun his way out of it

On November 22, 1994, Benny Lee Lawson once again went "downtown," this time on his own—this time with a Tech 9 assault pistol in his pocket.

In 1994, there was little or no security at police headquarters. You could take a Howitzer into police headquarters and no one would notice. Lawson found his way to the third floor and Lou Hennessy's office. He wanted Hennessy dead. He wanted to prove he was no snitch. He waited.

Hennessy was off that day. It was his first day off in months. He was in law school and had taken the day to study for a test. By 3:15 in the afternoon Lawson decided that he had waited long enough. He walked down the hallway and into the Cold Case squad room. There on the third floor, the slaughter began.

In rapid fire, bullets pierced the walls and the desks. Ambushed, the people inside had no real chance.

Dead: Sergeant Hank Daly, 51 years old.

Dead: Michael John Miller, 36 years old.

Dead: Martha Dixon Martinez, 35 years old.

It's been said that Martinez managed to get off a few shots and that Benny Lee Lawson used Martinez' gun to kill himself. They say he had a bullet wound to his eye.

FBI agent John David Kuchta was wounded in the attack. Shot in the chest, kidney, and stomach, he was flown to the hospital by a helicopter that had landed next door to the police headquarters building. John Kuchta recited the Hail Mary prayer over and over as he was flown Priority One to the trauma center. Over time he recovered and returned to work at the FBI. His prayers must have worked.

That day, November 22, 1994, signaled the beginning of an all-out war on the First and Kennedy Street Crew. The FBI and DC police began rounding up Crew members and, before it was over, had them all arrested and jailed and prosecuted for 17 murders, including the murders "downtown". Agents even went to Tanzania to arrest Kobi Mowat, the Crew's leader.

Over time, Mowat changed his opinion of Benny Lee Lawson. At his sentencing, Mowat gave this tribute to Lawson: "He represented me to the fullest. He will be my man, my comrade, for life."

The Washington police headquarters now carries the name of Hank Daly. But no one calls it the Daly building. And the names of Miller and Martinez—only their families and colleagues remember their sacrifices on that deadly day in the city of Washington.

5

LIFE IN SERIES AND OTHER INTERESTING BITS

JERRY GROSSMAN AND GIRLS GALORE

When Jerry Grossman drove a car, his hands were on the wheel at ten and two, just where they were supposed to be. Jerry was one of the most stable, reliable, dependable, careful men I have ever known in television. For many years, he was the producer of Channel 9's 11-o'clock Eyewitness News. Jerry checked and double-checked everything. In his reign as the late-night producer, we never had to unkill someone. Jerry ate the same thing for dinner every night, a turkey sandwich on white, carryout from Babe's across the street from the station. And Jerry held his own as left fielder on the station's softball team.

I tell you all of this because of an out-of-the-box experience I shared with Jerry many years ago.

Jerry Grossman loved music—rock 'n' roll music—and he came up with this idea to do a series, "So You Want to Be a Rock and Roll Star."

Really, Jerry? That's the kind of thing done in LA but not here in button-down, starch-shirted Washington, DC.

"No," said Jerry, "we can do it here. I wrote a song and I want you to sing it." And then . . . . Jerry called his song "Girls Galore." Here are some of its lyrics:

You broke my heart,
Tore it apart.
My eyes they cried so long,
You called me things,
Clipped my wings,
How come you've done me
wrong?

Honey, I got girls galore.
They line up
Outside my door.
Phone ringing off the hook.
Take my number out of the
book.
Don't even take a second
look.

My life is wild,
My life is free.
Ten women fill my future,
They dance and sing.
They question one thing:
They ask about your picture.

Dum do dee, dum do dee, dum do dee, dum.

That's how the whole thing started: Jerry and his song and me. I would be Fabian. Jerry would be Dick Clark. Fabian, a tone-deaf rock star invented by the industry, an American Bandstand favorite. If none of this makes sense to you, get Googling.

The boss gave Jerry permission to run with his dream and told him to make some interesting television out of it.

Now, before you get too judgmental, remember that we did this during the disco years. If it had a beat and you could dance to it, you had a hit. Maybe.

Jerry found a local DC music producer, Matt Allen, a song doctor, to mix Girls Galore and make me sound like a singer. Not only could I not carry a tune, I'm not sure I could push one

Matt said he had a cure for that, but first I had to practice and practice and practice. Matt arranged the music and cobbled together a band and had me sing Girls Galore over and over and over again. We filmed every take and retake and re-re-retake. We did it during work hours; we did it after work hours. Matt brought in a backup group named Tenderness fill in with vocals.

After about two weeks of rehearsals, I still sounded like a wounded duck. "Don't worry," said Matt, "we'll fix that in the studio."

Jerry was there for every off-keynote I sang, every shrill and animal sound I made. I was the singer but make no mistake—it was Jerry's song. He wanted to make sure everything came out just right.

Before my brief flirtation with the music business doing Girls Galore, I had no idea how music was made. I figured a band would play, a guy would sing, someone would record it, and that would be that. Out would roll a record or cassette of that very recording. How wrong I was.

At the studio, each musician played his part individually and each was recorded on one of many tracks through a control board with all sorts of dials and switches, like something out of The Wizard of Oz.

Then came my turn – to sing Girls Galore. I had memorized the words, but the tune—that was something else. Matt had me sing the song over and over and over, sometimes one line at a time. Through the mixer he double tracked my voice to give it texture and used Tenderness to smooth things out. Finally, finally we had a song.

How good was it? We put it to the test. Jerry arranged for the Plum, a big-time DC disco, to put Girls Galore on the playlist. Our cameras were there rolling as those all-too-familiar words, "Honey, I got girls galore," came blasting out of the nightclub's speakers.

It was a rush to see people dancing to our song. There was talk that a big record company was interested. But that went away.

In the music business, it's not all sunglasses and limousines.

Girls Galore made it onto the news. The story about how to make a rock 'n' roll record was edited by Dave Ewing, who spent a week matching shots and words and music. It was one of the longest stories ever aired in our newscasts: 7 minutes and 15 seconds. The bosses did something TV stations rarely do: They cut out commercial breaks so Girls Galore could run uncut without overriding the news stories of the day.

Jerry Grossman won an Emmy for that series.

Jerry went on to accomplish many more things in television, but I will bet you that today that Emmy is lit and on display somewhere in his house.

My daughter, Salley, chose Girls Galore for the Daddy/Daughter dance at her wedding.

Girls Galore was part of a multi part TV series on the business of rock and roll. It included interviews with Dick Clark, Cher, Greg Allman, and Peaches and Herb, plus a behind-the-scenes piece on a Beach Boys concert.

The series included the first interview with Brian Wilson after his long self-imposed sabbatical during which he spent a lot of time composing music in a sandbox at his California home. I asked Bryan something like this: How do you go from concert to concert night after night? His reply was something like this: I just go out and play that piano. I just play that goddamn piano. There was some painful honesty there.

NEWS SERIES AT CHANNEL 9 IN WASHINGTON

Three parters, five parters, series were a staple of local television news. They usually appeared magically during a rating period as a way to attract viewers and boost the numbers stations use to sell advertising. A series gave reporters extra time and resources to do some creative story telling.

It was 1974. The murder count in DC 295 a new record. At Channel 9 News, we decided to take a closer look at gun violence.

DC GENERAL

We arranged to spend the night in the emergency room with Dr. Patricia Fox at DC General Hospital. Before long a gunshot victim was rushed to the hospital. He didn't have far to go. He ran an auto repair shop nearby and was shot during a robbery at the shop. We were there as the surgical team moved with military-like precision to save the man's life. There was blood, a lot of blood. There was pain. There was the saving of his life. It was a powerful scene followed by an insightful interview with the emergency room doctor.

For those in the news business, this story was shot on film by cameraman Kline Mengle. The lights in the emergency room were bright – very bright. There was a mixture of tone and temperature of light as you moved from place to place. Instead of having his partner, Bruce Buckholtz, use a light to illuminate the scene, which would have washed out the picture, Mengle walked the entire emergency room, the doorway, the hallway, the treatment center, and the surgical area before the shoot. As he did so, he wrote down the appropriate f-stops for each area. Then, as he moved from place to place during the filming, he had Bruce whisper the proper f-stop settings into his ear. It worked perfectly.

HITTING THE STREETS

We wanted to document the last murder of 1974 in Washington. It was unusual to have a three-man crew on a story, but for that job we had a cameraman, a sound man, and a light man. It was New Year's Eve. Some of the crew had changed their plans to work this story.

We arranged to hit the streets with the DC Police Homicide Squad. We had no idea what we would find or where we would find it. We went to the far end of Washington, here and there hovering nearby likely shooting scenes.

Hours passed. Nothing.

Then came the call. A shooting on Tilden street northwest, blocks away from the Channel 9 studios. We raced to the scene – a parking garage in an upscale apartment building. The victim 78-year-old South Trimble, Jr., an attorney known for his involvement with the investigation of the 1937 Hindenburg crash. Mr. Trimble and his wife were returning home from a New Year's Eve Mass. Mr. Trimble dropped his wife off at the apartment building door. He then parked his car in the garage Mr. Trimble was getting out of the car police believe he was approached by a robber demanding money. When Mr. Trimble didn't respond the robber shot him dead. Mr. Trimble was hard of hearing, he may not have heard the robber's demand for money.

Because of our arrangement with the Homicide Squad we were allowed inside the police tape and got a close up view as detectives worked, gathering clues and evidence.

Then came a surprise: In the parking garage was the Catholic bishop. He had heard about the shooting and came to give Mr. Trimble the Last Rites. For a short time this bloody murder scene was transformed into a holy place.

Mr. Trimble's murder was never solved.

A PHONY ID

I got a phony ID, went to Virginia, and bought a handgun and a box of ammo in less than an hour. Then, in broad daylight I did a standup news cast, gun in hand, at the intersection of Wisconsin Avenue and Brandywine Street. It caused an uproar, and Ty Brown, a lawyer for Channel 9, intervened. There followed a not-so-ceremonial surrender of my weapon.

DOWN UNDER

We got a real inside look at the construction of the DC Metro system. Our cameras went beneath the Potomac River as workers dug the subway tunnel with a gigantic machine that gnawed away rock formations. The conditions were difficult; the filming was difficult. Down under it was quite an "undertaking."

GIVE AND TAKE

We got a tip that some of the charities in our city were something less than charitable – that they were diverting money intended for the needy into the pockets of the charities' administrators. We investigated these charities. We investigated other so-called charities with suspicious movements of money.

In the end, our investigation helped persuade the officials who were supposed to oversee charities in

Washington, DC to become more vigilant, to tighten their rules, and to enforce them more diligently.

NEWS SERIES AT CHANNEL 7 IN CHICAGO

The Honesty Test

We purchased 10 little boy wallets. You know the ones with little horses embedded on their sides and that you zipped up. In each wallet we put an ID card with a phone number in one pocket, a few baseball cards in another pocket, and a ten-dollar bill in the money compartment. On the bill we wrote a message that went something like this: 'Happy Birthday, Tommy. Love, Uncle Roy'.

Then, with cameras stationed on a high balcony, we dropped the wallets on a Chicago street. We then waited. And waited. One guy picked up a wallet, opened it up, took the money and tossed the wallet into a trash can.

Less than half of the people who picked up the wallets called the number and turned the wallets in. We gave rewards to those who did. They included a young child and a woman who was working two jobs. Those who didn't turn the wallets you might say they got their money a different way.

Horror In Hollywood

Off I went to Hollywood to discover the science of scary. I learned that the biggest scare in the movie is the first, which is designed to keep you in a high state of goose bumps waiting for something even worse.

I interviewed Linda Blair. Her head wasn't spinning that day, but her head spinning scene in the Exorcist still gives me the chills.

A makeup artist transformed my face into something very scary. It didn't take long.

Some doctors wired me up to an EKG machine and showed me some frightening scenes to measure my reaction. I don't think it worked well with my eyes closed.

The Bloody Mary Blood Test

This was my homage to the department of weights and measures. Under cover, I went from hotel to hotel and bar to bar ordering Bloody Marys. I ordered them at some of the most popular establishments in Chicago

After each drink was delivered to me, I deposited it into a, plastic pouches being careful not to let the ice contaminate the specimen. We sent the samples to a lab, yes a lab, for analysis. I even bought some Bloody Mary miniatures from the liquor store, emptied them into plastic pouches and sent them off.

I can report that we discovered that not all of the Marys were created equal. Which Mary had the most vodka? I'll be honest; I can't remember. It was 40 years ago, and I can't find the tape. I can tell you, though, that the Bloody Mary you make at home would likely be the winner. Cheers!

NEWS SERIES AT CHANNEL 7 IN DC: CONTEST TIME

Pat's Prized Pets

This was a contest for the most unusual pet and the best pet trick.

The prize was a golden super dooper pooper scooper.

The Winners: The most unusual pet was a pet pig that, despite his nearly 150 pounds of pork, roamed around the house, well, like a pig. The best pet trick was performed by a dog that opened a refrigerator door and brought his owner a beer.

Punch In With Pat

This was a contest for the best job, the worst, job, the most boring job.

The prize was a golden colored lunch pail.

The Winners included a septic system sucker, a raisin counter in a bread factory, and Vice President of the United States. I'll let you match the winners and the categories.

Plug In With Pat

This was a contest for the best Christmas display. Needless to say, we conducted it right before Christmas.

The prize was a golden extension cord

The Winners included big moving displays usually found in the suburbs and a lone house with one lone bulb.

Mishap at the Awards

We announced the winners of our contests with great fanfare.

At the Crampton Auditorium at Howard University we had show business lights and beautiful actresses and models showcase the awards. I wanted more; I wanted atmosphere. So, one time I added a smoke machine which we rented from a nearby theater supply house. It worked beautifully, creating the desired heavenly atmosphere and a real ooh and ahh affect . . .

until . . .

until . . .

until that oil-based smoke machine coated the entire stage and front seats with a sticky film. The cleanup was costly and the episode taught me a valuable lesson: heaven comes with a price.

NEWS SERIES AT CHANNEL 4 IN DC

Hardly Working

We wanted to see how city and county workers in the DC metro area spent their day on the job. We randomly selected the workers/work crews to follow and followed them from the time they left their yards in their trucks in the morning until they returned to the yards at the end of their shifts. All the time we secretly filmed their movements or – in a number of cases – lack of movement. It was a big undertaking. To avoid detection, we used rental cars and assigned two different undercover vehicles to each work crew.

We followed one Montgomery, Maryland 'work' crew that left the yard right on time and went directly to a diner. There they sat for more than hour before moving on to a job site.

We followed a sewer truck in Arlington. The crew put out orange safety cones and then they parked – just parked. They sat there and sat there. And then sat there some more. ALL DAY LONG.

In the District we followed a 'worker' in a big city truck who left the yard, drove to a liquor store, went inside, and returned to his truck with a large bottle in a brown paper bag. He then drove into a residential neighborhood where a woman climbed into the front seat. And there the truck remained. At times the woman disappeared from sight. Later she left the truck, and the man drove back to the yard. Not much "work" done that day.

We showed video of our findings to the workers' supervisors; we understand their annual job reviews didn't go well.

Hottest Ticket In Town

As I write this story the Washington Football Team (WFT) is in the dump – last in the NFC East. Tickets for home games are selling for as little as four dollars a seat. You can't even go to movie for that.

There was a time, though, a glorious time, when the WFT made the playoffs and won Super Bowls, when getting tickets to a WFT game was an expensive, if not an impossible, quest. There was a season ticket waiting list with hundreds of hopeful people in the queue. It was during that time that we did this story.

Our story started with a list – the list of WFT ticket holders leaked to us by a man in the know. We found businesses with scores of tickets. We found season ticket holders that had been dead for years, their families paying for and receiving what you might call ghost season tickets. The most surprising thing we found, though, was the secret and *very long* waiting list. We found people who, from year to year, actually went down the list instead of advancing up the list. They might be 151 on the list one year and 171 the next year. How could that happen?

Jack Kent Cooke, the WFT's then owner, did not take kindly to our series about the treasured tickets. The Squire, as some called him, had an army of lawyers who went on the attack before we aired the first story. Our lawyers were prepared for it. With each piece we ran we included a disclaimer to the effect that the WFT is a private company that could sell tickets to whomever they pleased.

It was a most popular series about the haves and have nots at a time when a WFT game was the place to be.

The Hot Car Hit List

Washington television used to have a news mantra: There were three stories about which you couldn't go wrong: the weather, the traffic, and the WFT.

I did a lot of series involving lists, including a series about hot – stolen – cars.

What cars did thieves target? Mostly Japanese.

How did they steal the cars? Using a screwdriver.

How they get rid of the stolen autos? They cut them up and sold the parts

Cars now have car alarms and other safety features designed to thwart car thieves. Even with these, cars are stolen, often from people who simply fail to lock their doors or who leave their cars idling while they run into a 7-11 for a cup of coffee.

Driving Me Crazy

We did another series on the most dangerous intersections in and around Washington DC. Statistics indicated that the intersection of Bladensburg Road and New York Avenue in the District's Northeast quadrant was the most dangerous in the City. To test the accuracy of the statistics, we stationed a camera at each corner of the intersection.

Before long. BAM. Point made.

Dying To Drive

Teenagers were being killed in accidents on the roadways in what seemed to be large numbers. We aired our conversations with the cops and teenagers' relatives. Most importantly we aired our conversations with teenagers, both those who had been involved in an accident and those who had not. The conversations were compelling and insightful. It's not like this topic hadn't been addressed before, but to me it seemed different this time. I hope it made a difference.

Collins, Brenner, and Buchanan

MIKE BUCHANAN

The Sting

For Mike "Buck" Buchanan, a taquito at 7-Eleven was a destination lunch.

For Mike "Buck" Buchanan, the dashboard of his car was a notepad.

For Mike "Buck" Buchanan, a deadline was only a suggestion.

Mike Buchanan was one of the best television police reporters in the city of Washington. Most cops don't trust reporters. I think there is a course in cop school—the "Don't Talk to Reporters" course, followed by the "Never Talk to Reporters" course. But cops talked to Buck. They trusted Buck. And that paid off big time for Mike Buchanan. Oftentimes he would walk into the homicide squad and read a report as a detective was typing it. At crime scenes the police would escort Buck behind police lines to hear the briefings that were usually reserved for high-ranking officers.

You see, Buck spent time with cops not just when he needed information. He would hang out with them just to see how things were going. He would meet with them and talk with them over drinks, dinner, and coffee. He sympathized with them; he knew how hard their jobs were. Buck valued – and worked – his relationships with the police. The cops knew Buck was golden.

Back in the '70s, the DC police pulled off one of the most creative operations in the history of Washington crime. They called it "The Sting." Police officers posed as mob guys in town to buy stolen goods. The architect, a cop named Robert Arscott, set it up in a warehouse section of Northeast Washington. Thieves, killers, and other crooks lined up to offload their ill-gotten gains. Arscott even had a cop pose as "the Don." He sat in a throne-like chair, and crooks kissed his ring as they came in to cut a deal. Not all crooks negotiated good deals with "the Don." Some of them made downright stupid deals. For instance, one crook sold "the Don" a brand-new car he had just stolen from a dealership for a couple of hundred dollars. During The Sting, the police recovered $5.5 million in stolen goods, arrested 365 crooks, and closed 1,800 cases. Whew!

At the time of The Sting, Buck and I were known as "Muck and Mire" or "Page One and Page Two" at Channel 9. The Sting was perfect for us, but there was one problem: when big bust was going down, Buck was getting married in Oklahoma. I was supposed to be the best man in the wedding. Instead I was his best man back in Washington. On his wedding day, Buck phoned back tips on The Sting so that we could get the video and information we needed to get the edge on all the other stations. Buck's honeymoon? He spent it in Washington doing follow-ups on The Sting.

Cojones Muy Grande

On March 30, 1981, President Reagan was shot and wounded at the Washington Hilton Hotel. From the time of the shooting, the City was all abuzz; reporters from everywhere, from every news organizations worked the story top to bottom. They wanted to know about the President, of course, but they also wanted to know everything else. Who was the shooter and why did he do it? How was it possible for the shooter to get close enough to the President with a gun to shoot him? Was there a mastermind behind the shooter? And more.

Mike Buchanan knew the answers. He knew John Hinckley was the shooter. He knew how many shots Hinckley fired. He knew the type of gun Hinckley used. More importantly, Buck knew the motive: Hinckley shot Reagan because he wanted to impress actress Jodie Foster. Now imagine being a reporter and going to your boss and saying the guy who tried to kill the President of the United States was just trying to impress an actress. It took some cojones to go on the air with a story like that, but Buck had them and did it, and he was right as rain. That story was broadcast not just around the City but around the world.

The Tarot Card Tip

During the Sniper attacks in Washington, it was Buck who broke the story about the death card left at a school by one of the gunmen. It had the ominous message, "Call me God." It also had a fingerprint that later linked one of the shooters to the murders.

From 1970 until 2003 Buck worked at Channel 9 when it was WTOP then WDVM then WUSA. He was a reporter and anchor he did everything at that station except Mass for the Shut-Ins.

It wasn't always about crime.

Buck covered politics. He danced on TV one night with candidate Arthur Fletcher after Fletcher lost the mayoral election.

Buck covered sports. He went to all the Redksins' Super Bowls. They are still working on his expense accounts.

And Buck went traveling ..In a beat-up old sedan with "Mike on the Road" hand painted on the side Buck went from place to place doing stories that would make Charles Kurwalt blush.

Off Duty And Off-Course

Golf. Buck and I were best of friends. We vacationed together. We gambled together. We performed godfather duties for each other's children. We played golf together. Our golf was nothing like the game you see on television. We didn't just have mulligans—if we both had bad shots (which was often), we would grant each other amnesty. I remember two incidents.

We were at the Rock Creek Golf Course, which only had a couple of sand traps at the time. While lining up a putt, Buck took one step back, then another step back, and then, he disappeared entirely – deep into the sand trap on his backside. The scene looked like one from The Awakening.

We were at the University of Maryland Golf Course, where some construction was going on near the clubhouse. Buck, who was uncharacteristically early for the tee time, decided to practice his putting. He walked to a green, dropped three balls, and began putting them around. Then came sharp shouts from nearby: "YOU MOVE AWAY! YOU BACK OFF! YOU GET BACK!" The shouts got louder, stronger, and damn near physical as a Korean foursome approached what turned out to be the 18th hole, which Buck had mistaken for a putting green. Buck did the only thing he could do: he bowed, sheepishly picked up his balls, and quickly and quietly backed away.

Racquetball. Buck and I had regular racquetball games at Bethesda Sport and Health. The sets were interspersed with cigarette breaks outside and lunch at McDonalds across the street. It wasn't exactly the image the athletic club had in mind.

Buck's eyesight was not exactly 20/20, especially without glasses. One day when he was in the locker room without his glasses and, shall we say, buck naked, he mistook the door to the pool for the door to the shower, backed in, and invented a swim stroke yet to be named.

Pong. Around the corner from the television station was a restaurant called the Dancing Crab, a seafood house. For many people in TV, it was our version of Cheers, a place where we would drink and unwind more often than we should. My wife had the phone number of the Dancing Crab memorized.

In a corner of the restaurant was Pong, one of the world's first full-sized video games, a little electronic ball that bounced back and forth in a hypnotic way. Buck and I became proficient at Pong and took on all challengers. Some wagering might have been involved. At the Dancing Crab, Buck and I make an important discovery, one that I remember to this day: Alcohol and Pong don't mix. We would crush early, get clobbered late. Yet another reason to go straight home after work.

Betting. Buck and I bet on football, college and pro. At casinos, Buck would dress up in a suit and pretend to be James Bond. At home we would play blackjack head-to-head for hours and hours until we were dead even. One New Year's we had an incredibly lucky streak. We bet virtually every bowl game and were 10 for 12. The bookie declared Chapter 11—even when we won, we lost.

Buck retied in 2012 and moved to Bethany Beach Delaware. There he got a job as a pit boss at a nearby casino. Finally, Buck was on the right side of the gambling game.

Michael Coe Buchanan died at his beach home April 16, 2020. He was 78 years old. He left a trail of memories that will not soon be forgotten.

6

COLD-BLOODED KILLERS

HENRY "LITTLE MAN" JAMES

The police headquarters in Washington is located at Third Street and Indiana Avenue, Northwest. The homicide squad is on the third floor. There was a time when reporters could move freely through the building, a time when, after an arrest in a homicide case, detectives would march the suspect down the hallway to be booked. That inglorious parade was called the "perp" (perpetrator) walk.

Back in 1991, I was on the third floor when the police marched Henry "Little Man" James down that hallway.

I shouted out to him: "Why did you kill her?"

No answer, just a big smirk. The Little Man, small, stocky, and arrogant, just kept walking down the dimly lit hallway.

"So what were you doing out there that night?"

"Just keeping my composure," James said.

Book him.

On November 16, 1991, Henry "Little Man" James shot and killed Patricia Lexie as she sat in the front seat of a car next to her husband. They had been married just 11 months. It was reported that James shot Lexie because he felt like killing somebody. It was reported that James shot Lexie because he wanted to see if his gun worked.

Henry "Little Man" James was 19 years old and the father of two children by two teenage girls. Lexie's murder was not his first serious brush with the law. When he murdered Lexie, he was already facing prison terms for two prior shootings. When he killed Lexie, he was free on bail.

Henry "Little Man" James was the terror of his Northeast neighborhood—so much so that scores of neighbors signed a petition asking the judge to keep James jailed pending his trial in the Lexie murder case.

After his trial, at which he was found guilty, and during his sentencing, the judge told James, "Simple justice requires that you never walk among us again."

MURDER BY THE BOOK

On March 3, 1993, I was on North Gate Drive in Silver Spring, Maryland as the terrible news spread. Friends and family members approached the scene doubled over in grief. There were tears and screams. Women fell to the ground. There was, in short, uncontrolled sorrow about what happened in the house nearby.

Three people were dead: Mildred Horn, 43, her quadriplegic eight-year old son, Trevor Horn, and Janice Roberts Saunders, 38, who was Trevor's nurse.

It didn't take long for police to zero in on a suspect or a motive.

Mildred Horn was estranged from her husband, Lawrence Horn, a former Motown music producer. Lawrence had set up a $1.7 million trust fund for Trevor following the botched medical procedure that left Trevor paralyzed. If Mildred and Trevor were dead, the trust money would revert to Lawrence. The family knew that. The police knew that. Lawrence Horn knew that.

Lawrence had an alibi. He said he was in Hollywood, California, thousands of miles from the scene, on the day of the murder.

During the investigation, detectives focused their attention on James Edward Perry, a street preacher who was one of Horn's old Motown friends and who was said to be Horn's spiritual advisor. Detectives suspected that Horn had hired Perry to kill his wife and child – that Perry was a minister turned murderer – and began monitoring the pair. Eventually the FBI got Horn's cousin to testify that he had acted as the go-between for Perry and Horn as they arranged the murders.

During our investigation we got a phone tip about a book that was said to be a primer for Perry on how to kill his targets: *Hit Man: A Technical Manual for Independent Contractors.* We found it. The book laid out everything needed for a murder: the best gun to use (a 22-caliber); how to guarantee success (shoot the victim in the eye); and how to cover your tracks. It was murder by the numbers.

Perry shot Mildred Horn and Janice Saunders in the eye, but he killed Trevor, cruelly and heartlessly, by disconnecting the breathing tubes that kept the little boy alive.

What Horn and Perry believed to be the perfect plot unraveled like a cheap sweater once the police found Horn's cousin and convinced him to talk. Lawrence Horn and James Perry were each sentenced to three life terms in prison. Both died there.

Mildred Horn's family sued the publisher of the Hit Man book. The publisher settled, but the settlement couldn't erase the pain from what happened on North Gate Drive on that March day.

COLONEL MUSTARD

That's what people in Georgetown called the guy prancing around in a military uniform, masquerading as a general—an unusual sight in this part of town. I was in Georgetown because of a murder. When I saw "the general" walking down the street in front of the murder house, cameraman Sean Casey and I followed in hot pursuit.

"What do you know? Tell me about what happened." We fired questions at him as we walked alongside and behind and sometimes in front of him down Wisconsin Avenue. We followed him into a restaurant, out of the restaurant, across Wisconsin Avenue, into an alley—until he disappeared behind a gate

It was August 11, 2011, and Viola Drath, a 91-year old woman, had been found dead in a second-floor bathroom of her three-story home in Georgetown. She had several broken ribs; bruises on her spine, head, chest, and arms; and scratches and bruises on her neck. Viola was missing a thumbnail. Police suspected that she had been strangled and had lost a thumbnail while trying to defend herself. Police suspected her husband, Albrecht Muth, the strange man we were pursuing. Of course, we didn't know all this when we first pursued him.

As we followed Muth we got a lot of video but little information.

This story begins with a most unusual wedding. It was 1990.

Viola Drath was the bride. She was 70, a journalist, a playwright, a socialite, and an activist on behalf of military mothers. She had a fashionable townhouse in the heart of Georgetown.

Albrecht Muth was the groom. He was a 26-year-old man of East German descent, an ambitious former congressional intern. At different times after his marriage to Viola, he assumed the persona of a U.S. Army officer, a count, a foreign spy, and an Iraqi general. At one point he wore an eye patch over one eye and claimed to have lost the eye while fighting as a mercenary in South America. The patch later disappeared.

Muth told prosecutors that his marriage to Viola was one of convenience. A year after the marriage, Muth pleaded guilty to assault for punching Viola in the face. Other assaults followed, but Viola declined to press charges.

Viola and Albrecht slept in the same room but in separate beds. She gave him an allowance of $2,000 a month. The marriage soured. Muth had a gay lover who also complained of abuse.

Muth first told police that Viola had died from a fall. Later he said she was killed by an Iranian assassin. Cops were unmoved by Muth's stories. They discovered that shortly after Viola's death Muth had done an on-line search for flights to Iceland and another search for information on border crossings into Mexico and Canada.

Albrecht Muth was charged with first-degree murder and jailed pending trial. His trial was all but usual. He participated in the trial by closed-circuit television from his hospital bed because his periodic fasting left him too weak to attend the trial.

Muth was represented by attorneys from the DC Public Defender Service, whom he subsequently fired. The Court permitted him to undertake his own defense but later withdrew its permission after he claimed that it was the Archangel Gabriel who had ordered him to fast.

Muth's unusual behavior led to a series of psychiatric exams and court hearings during which his attorneys argued that Muth was not mentally competent to stand trial and that he should be committed to St. Elizabeth's Hospital, DC's psychiatric hospital. The Court ruled that Muth was competent, and the case moved forward. The trial lasted six days, during which the defense argued that Muth had no reason to kill Viola because he would inherit nothing upon her death. Prosecutors argued that Muth fatally beat and strangled Drath during a drunken rage.

In January 2014, more than two and half years after Viola Drath's death, Albrecht Muth was found guilty of murder. He was sentenced to 50 years in prison.

AARON ALEXIS

September 16, 2013. It was bedlam. I was with cameraman Tarik Warner in a live truck. Something awful had happened at the Navy Yard. All the streets around the Navy Yard were blocked off. Emergency vehicles raced back and forth, their sirens blaring, lights flashing, radios crackling. Cops with long guns moved every which way. A wartime flashback: a helicopter swooping down rescuing people from a roof top.

There was a mass shooting at the Navy Yard. We got as close as we could and watched the action from about a block away. It was a scene of mass confusion:

- A 9-1-1 call for help came from the scene, Building 197. Building 197's address was not in the police 9-1-1 call system database, so the dispatcher sent the cops to the Navy Yard without identifying the building where the shooting occurred.
- When police got to the Navy Yard, the gates were locked. The security officers had left their posts and gone to the scene to hunt down the shooter.

- When police finally gained entry through a civilian gate, they had to ask people as they ran, "Where's Building 197?". People didn't know. They saw people running from a building and ran toward it. That's how they found the scene.

The shooter, Aaron Alexis, 34 years old, was a computer worker with "The Experts" project at the Navy Yard. He had a valid pass to enter the site. Alexis was from New York but had been raised in Texas. He had served four years in the Navy.

On the morning of the shooting Alexis drove onto the base in a rented Toyota Prius. He carried a disassembled, sawed-off shotgun into the building in a bag and snapped the gun together in a fourth-floor bathroom. Then the shooting rampage began.

He began shooting at 8:16 a.m. Four people were hit; three were dead. Alexis then shot and killed a security officer and took the officer's handgun. Floor by floor he weaved his way through the building as cops tried to hunt him down. Finally, the police cornered Alexis near a cubicle on the first floor. Out of shotgun shells, Alexis used the dead cop's handgun. A gun battle between Alexis and SWAT officer Dorian DeSantis took place at close range. DeSantis was hit in the chest but was saved by his flak vest. Alexis was hit—and hit again. And again. He fell to the floor. He was dead.

From start to finish, Alexis' shooting spree lasted one hour and nine minutes. In the end, twelve people were dead and three wounded.

Prior to the shooting, Alexis had complained that he heard voices, that he was controlled by low-frequency devices. On his gun he had scrawled, "Better off this way. My ELF weapon." ELF: Electronic Low Frequency.

The cops who rushed the building were credited for their bravery. One commander wrote, "Nobody flinched, nobody blinked."

Building 197 re-opened in February 2015. Everybody knows where it is now.

MIR AIMAL KANSI

It was June 15, 1997. Brad Garrett and two other FBI agents rushed into a suspect's hotel room. Garrett asked the guy, "What's your name?"

"Fuck you," the man said.

For Brad Garrett that vulgar reply was a start. Now he knew the man understood and spoke English. But was this the man for which he had searched all these years? Garrett wasn't sure. This man had a longer beard and was heavier than Garrett expected.

One of the agents wrestled the suspect to the floor; he screamed. Garrett said "We had to gag him. We didn't want to draw attention to what was going on." The agents cuffed him and then, in the small, dark room, they rolled him over. Agent Garrett pulled a fingerprint kit from his pocket and took the man's fingerprints. Using a flashlight and a magnifying glass, Garrett compared the prints. The whorls and ridges matched. "It's him," Garrett said. "It's him."

Garrett had been searching for CIA killer Mir Aimal Kansi for four years, five months, and 14 days. Finally, he had him cuffed and under arrest.

January 25, 1993: Cars lined up in two lanes to make a left turn into the CIA headquarters in McLean, Virginia. A man in a pickup truck, stopped in one of the lanes, took out an AK-47, and fired into the cars waiting to make that turn. Two people killed outright and another three wounded. Twenty-Eight-year-old Frank Darling was hit multiple times. The bullets splintered his skull. The shooter was Mir Aimal Kansi, a Pakistani who was angered by the CIA's influence in the Middle East. At the time, no one knew anything about Kansi or why he did what he did.

Following the shooting, Kansi got back into his truck, drove to a nearby park, grabbed the AK-47, walked into the woods, and waited. And waited. After about an hour and a half, when he heard no sirens and saw no cops, he figured the coast was clear. He drove his truck to his apartment in Herndon, hid the murder weapon in a green trash bag, got something to eat at McDonald's, then went to see a friend. He paid cash for a plane ticket to Pakistan and returned the next day to his homeland.

Kansi's escape was made easy because the police weren't looking for a truck; they were looking for a car, a witness having told them the shooter was driving a car. When you're looking down the barrel of an assault rifle, you don't always see things clearly. Remember, this happened long before the age of the surveillance cameras make it almost impossible for movements around secure facilities to go unnoticed.

Early on Investigators knew three things:

- The CIA was the target.
- The shooter was a lone man.
- The shell casings at the scene were from an AK-47, and there were fingerprints on those shell casings.

A task force comprising agents from the CIA, the FBI, and the ATF was formed. They set up a command center at the Fairfax County, Virginia Police Headquarters. Brad Garrett, a special FBI agent, was a team member. Though he worked on the side of the angels, Garrett always dressed in black. He had a reputation for solving the unsolvable. This case was a real stumper even for Garrett.

Garrett said that, in shooting incidents like this, the gunman usually purchases the weapon a short time before the assault. With the help of the ATF, the team reviewed all the purchases of AK-47s from gun shops in the year prior to the shooting. In Maryland, approximately 300 had been sold. In Virginia, the number was close to a thousand. It took about a week before they hit pay dirt.

The agents discovered that the Blue Ridge Arsenal in Virginia had sold an AK-47 on January 22, 1993, just three days before the CIA murders. The man who purchased that weapon: Mir Aimal Kansi.

Investigators went to Kansi's garden apartment in Herndon, where they found the murder weapon hidden beneath a couch. Kansi's roommate said he remembered Kansi purchasing the weapon. In a closet they found a handgun, ammunition, and passport photos of Kansi. Now they had a fingerprint, a weapon, and a photo—but no Kansi.

The team launched an international manhunt. Garrett traveled around the world following up on leads and tips and sightings. The team circulated fliers with Kansi's photo; at one point they put Kansi's picture on matchbooks and passed them around Pakistan. Years went by. The case got cold, but the U.S. never stopped looking for Kansi. It offered a reward – a gigantic reward – for information leading to Kansi's capture. (The award amount is classified.) The reward worked, capturing the attention of people who knew Kansi.

The team wanted the capture to be perfect; Garrett wanted the capture to be perfect. A latent-fingerprint specialist trained Garrett to take and read fingerprints "on the road." Garrett and the other agents practiced room entry so that they wouldn't shoot each other if things went sideways. They practiced everything, anticipating what could go wrong. Finally, they were ready.

They flew to Pakistan. Then came the setup at the Hotel Shalimar. The agents planned to make their move at 4 a.m. based upon the assumption that people would still be asleep at that time of day and that, consequently, Kansi's capture wouldn't draw much attention or cause much of a stir. That assumption was wrong. You see, in June Pakistan is insufferably hot. To avoid the inferno-like afternoon heat, Pakistanis work from 4:00 a.m. till noon. When the FBI team showed up at the hotel, it was like rush hour, Pakistani style. So much for the early-morning discreet strategy.

Nevertheless, the takedown went on as scheduled. The informant (now a wealthy informant) led the team to Kansi's third-floor hotel room and knocked on the door to awaken Kansi for morning prayers. When Kansi opened the door, Garrett and his agents made their move. This is where we started this story.

After verifying Kansi's identity, the agents pulled a light, burlap-like hood over Kansi's head (apparently that's Pakistani arrest procedure) and led him from the hotel to an SUV. Kansi leaned over to Garrett and asked, "You're going to take me back to America, aren't you?" Garrett replied: "That's a possibility."

The agents took Kansi to a safe house and placed him in a cell. Garrett and the two other agents took turns sitting next to his cell for two days as they made arrangements to extract Kansi from Pakistan. There was a snag, a Presidential intervention, and then a flight in an unmarked military plane to Dulles Airport in Virginia. The plane re-fueled midair to avoid having to land to fuel. The flight took approximately 15 hours. A helicopter met the flight at Dulles and transported Kansi to a Fairfax, Virginia jail, where he was held pending trial. Once Kansi was locked up in Fairfax, Garrett took a step back. But he didn't stay away.

After Kansi was convicted and sentenced to death, Garrett visited him in prison, sometimes sitting outside his death-row cell. "He called me Mr. Brad, I called him Aimal," Garrett recalled. "He trusted me. I always told him the truth, told him what was going to happen. No bullshit. I was the only person he knew. He said he didn't have any money in his canteen fund. I put in $100 dollars so he could get things like a toothbrush and toothpaste."

Kansi invited Garrett to his execution. Not many killers ask their arresting officer to accompany them to their execution. On November 14, 2002, Garrett was at the Greensville Correctional Facility in Virginia. He had arrived the day before and stayed at a nearby hotel. He went to Kansi's cell and quietly stepped back as he watched Kansi rocking back and forth, chanting prayers over and over again. Garrett was there as Kansi was led to the death chamber, as he was strapped to a table, and as tubes were inserted in his arms. On the other side of a glass wall there was a gallery of witnesses.

"No god is greater than Allah!" Kansi cried out.

The death drugs were injected into the tubes.

Mir Aimal Kansi gasped and died.

He met with death almost ten years after he delivered it at the CIA.

"It was weird," Garrett said. " It bothered me a lot. I couldn't sleep that night. I felt that way for a number of days."

TERROR IN WASHINGTON

It's rare for a reporter to cover a story that rolls on from year to year with so much hate and bloodshed. The story that I am about to relate covers murders that occurred in 1973 and retaliatory take overs that occurred in 1977. I covered the murder scene, the police investigation that followed, and the arrest and conviction of the men responsible. Years later I covered the acts of retaliation for those murders and the trials of the people behind them. I believe that retaliation was the first terrorist attack in Washington.

The story begins with a real estate deal.

Before Morton's or Ruth's Chris, the only place to get a real belly-buster steak was Cannon's, a well-known restaurant in the Florida Avenue market, an active, thriving center of commerce in Northeast Washington.

Chicken farmers sold, butchered, and defeathered birds right there on the spot. Meat men in long, white, bloodstained coats carved up Prime and Choice cuts of beef to order. Farmers sold fresh produce off the back of their trucks. Fancy restaurant chefs, corner-store grocers, and everyday people would snake their way through the various stalls and stores looking for the deal of the day. In the midst of it all was Cannon's, a large, no-frills place with the best food. The owner/operator: Rita Cannon.

When chain supermarkets invaded DC, places like the Florida Avenue market began to fade and so did Cannon's popularity. I'm not sure if that's what prompted Rita Cannon to sell her house, an impressive stone structure on 16th Street, Northwest, in a classy neighborhood known as the Gold Coast. In 1971, though, that's what she did. The man who bought the house was as impressive as the house he bought: Milwaukee Bucks basketball star Kareem Abdul Jabbar.

Why would a Milwaukee basketball player buy a house in DC?

Kareem used to go by the name Lew Alcindor. In high school he played for Power Memorial in New York, a team that held the record for the longest high-school win streak in the country. (By the way, that winning streak was broken by Washington's DeMatha High in a game that drew national TV coverage. But I'm getting way off track here.)

In 1970, Lew Alcindor became Kareem Abdul Jabbar after a man known as Hammas Abdul Khaalis converted him to the Hanafi Muslim Movement. The next year, Kareem bought Rita's 16th Street house so it could be used as headquarters for the Hanafi sect.

That house would soon become a killing ground.

To understand this story, you need to know a bit about Hamaas Abdul Khaalis. Before Khaalis was a Muslim, he was a Seventh Day Adventist and before that a Roman Catholic. He was born in Gary, Indiana in 1921; his name was Ernest Timothy McGhee. McGhee served in the military but was discharged on grounds of mental instability. He was a talented jazz drummer who played with some of the greats. McGhee converted to Sunni Muslim and then infiltrated the Black Muslims, which were then known as the Nation of Islam. He rose through the Black Muslim ranks and became close to the Black Muslims' leader, Elijah Muhammad, so close that McGhee thought he was in line to succeed Muhammad.

In 1957, though, McGhee lost influence and split with the Black Muslims. The split was bitter. Khaalis sent dozens of letters to all the Nation of Islam mosques, accusing Muhammad of deceiving and robbing people and dooming them to hell. The year after Khaalis left the Black Muslims, he formed the Hanafi Movement and took the Sunni Muslim name Hammas Abdul Khaalis. In 1972, Khaalis published an additional letter attacking the Nation of Islam and its beliefs.

On January 18, 1973, two men appeared at the front door of that big house on 16th Street. They said they wanted to buy some Hanafi literature. Daud, Khaalis' son, opened the door. With guns drawn the two rushed into the house. Five more gunmen followed them inside. Shots were fired; Daud was shot and killed at close range.

It didn't stop there.

The gunmen forced Khaalis' wife, Bibi, to watch as they drowned two children in an upstairs bathtub. Then, in the basement, they forced her to watch as they drown Khaalis' nine-day-old granddaughter in a laundry tub. They bound Bibi and shot her eight times. A gunman shot Khaalis' daughter Amina three times and were trying to finish her off when his gun jammed. She survived, but she was so traumatized by what she saw, that her later testimony was of no value.

The gunmen escaped. Later they were identified as members of a Black Muslim group in Philadelphia. They were brought back to DC, tried, and convicted. I covered the murders, and I covered the trials.

Khaalis was shopping when the Black Muslims slaughtered his family at the Hanafi house. He never recovered from what happened there. I drove by the house and watched the Hanafis marching back and forth like palace guards with swords at the ready. It was medieval. Khaalis' hatred grew daily like a festering sore. He vowed to get revenge. He vowed to do something; he planned that something. It took four years, but Khaalis found a way to avenge his loss.

Khaalis and his followers launched a three-pronged attack—a coordinated take over first of the B'nai B'rith Building then the Islamic Center, and then the District Building.

With military-like precision, Khaalis and six armed followers stormed the B'nai B'rith headquarters. They corralled 100 hostages, beating some, taunting others. Khaalis ranted that Jews control the courts, Jews control the press. His hatred was so great that he had lost control of himself.

As police respond to the B'nai B'rith, three Hanafi soldiers take over the Islamic Center and took eleven hostages. Of all the takeovers, the Islamic Center was the least violent, but it was scary, nonetheless.

Then two gunmen rushed to the fifth floor of the District Building, the place where the city council meets, the place where the mayor meets, the place where reporters covering the city meet. They wanted a big-name hostage. It got ugly fast. Maurice Williams, a WHUR reporter, was shot dead as he stepped off the elevator. He was just 24 years old. Security officer Mack Cantrell was shot and wounded and later died of a heart attack. Marion Barry, then a councilman, was hit in the chest by a shotgun pellet and rescued by a cop named Ike Fulwood. In a way, this wounding helped advance Barry's mayoral campaign. It didn't hurt Fulwood, either, later Mayor Marion Barry made Fullwood chief of police.

The whole siege lasted about 38 hours. Local television stations gave it wall-to-wall coverage. Khaalis knew some of the local news anchors, and he called them to make demands. He wanted a number of things. Most of all he wanted the killers of his family released to him. He wanted an-eye-for-an-eye justice. He wanted people to feel his hurt.

But for a couple of things, the siege could have lasted longer and been more deadly:

First, Joe O'Brien, the homicide detective who got to know Khaalis when he worked the murders at the Hanafi house, spoke to Khaalis and calmed him.

Next, Ambassadors from Iran, Egypt, and Pakistan pleaded with Khaalis to end the sieges without additional bloodshed.

Finally, Police Chief Maurice Cullinane took off his gun, went to Khaalis, and personally cut a deal: Surrender, and you won't go to jail; you will be charged, and then you and your followers will be allowed to go back to the Hanafi house. Khaalis took the offer. The gunmen released the hostages and surrendered. The City was safe again.

Following the surrender, Khaalis and his men were booked and charged and then allowed to return to the Hanafi house, where they remained under house arrest until their trials.They were convicted on multiple charges. Khaalis died in prison in November 2003. The house on 16th Street still belongs to the Hanafis. It sits right nearby a synagogue.

NINE-ELEVEN

September 11, 2001 was a beautiful day in Washington DC. The weather was perfect; the sun was shining; the sky was blue. It was my 30th wedding anniversary. I had taken the entire week off and had planned to play some golf and do some day trips. I had arranged for my wife, Emily and me, to have a special, romantic dinner at the Oceanaire Restaurant. That morning I was watching television and saw a plane fly into the north tower of the World Trade Center and, minutes later, a second plane fly into the south tower of the World Trade Center. I went to work.

On that morning, NBC4 reporter Megan McGrath and her cameraman, John Greenwood, were sitting in a live truck in the Ballston section of Arlington County, Virginia, waiting to cover their first story of the day, a preview of a new commuter bus line. As they waited, they watched the Today Show and saw what I had seen.

For years Megan McGrath had been the early-morning reporter for NBC4 in Washington. It was not an easy job. Generally, it involved covering murders and car accidents, standing in the dark talking about things that happened the night before or something that might happen after the sun comes up. When you're the morning reporter, you're always in the dark, always sleep deprived. It takes a certain kind of talent—you have to be fast, glib, and journalistically agile. Megan was, and is, all those things. It's in her DNA: Her father, Patrick McGrath, was a highly regarded Washington anchor and reporter for years.

After the planes hit the twin towers, Megan and John were directed to go to National Airport to do a sidebar story on security. The route from Ballston to the airport took McGrath close by the Pentagon.

Megan heard it before she saw it—a loud but muffled noise, like a huge fist pounding into a pillow. A gigantic fireball rose into the clear blue sky. Megan said that, for a brief moment, it was like all of the air had been sucked out of the live truck. Later she said, "There was no question in my mind what happened. It was a plane into the Pentagon. I began cussing like a sailor, my hands shaking so badly I couldn't dial the phone."

The live truck pulled into a nearby gas station. People ran from the Pentagon. Cellphone service jammed, causing McGrath and Greenwood to go old-school and use old-fashioned two-way radios to get on the air. As they did that, an MP raced to the truck and yelled at them: "Move! MOVE! MOVE!." He told them to take cover—that there was another plane coming in.

"Another plane coming in!" That's the message I heard on the police radio as I made my way downtown. There was another target—a fourth target. Maybe the Capitol. Maybe the White House. Everyone was on high alert.

Downtown DC was like a scene from a cheap horror movie – there was a mass exodus from the City. People who were frightened to use the subway walked for miles to get out of the City. Some stores had televisions in their windows, and every so often crowds gathered in knots to watch before they continued their journeys.

Cellphones were useless. Airports were closed down. Hours and days would go by before families were safely reunited. But for many families there would be no reunion—just a great sense of sorrow and loss.

Every year on September 11 Megan McGrath is called back to that spot near the Pentagon to retell her story, and every year on that day, she says, "I get jumpy as a cat."

THE SNIPERS

It was 2002. Everyday people doing ordinary things around the region were being shot for no apparent reason—gunned down by sniper fire. The shootings appeared to be random. For three weeks, just about everyone was ducking for cover.

People knelt on the ground at gas stations as they filled up their cars. They ran from grocery stores to their cars with only the items they could carry in their hands. Schools cancelled recess. Athletic games were postponed.

No one lingered outside.

When it began, cops had no clue. On October 2, there was a shot into a Michael's craft store in Aspen Hills. It came close to a cashier, but no one was injured. Then, about an hour later and a short distance away a man was shot in a grocery store parking lot. The bullet seemed to come from nowhere. There were no witnesses. There seemed to be no motive. Nothing.

The next day, a chain of death: A man mowing a lawn in Rockville. A woman sitting on a bench outside a Crisp & Juicy Chicken joint. A cabdriver fueling his taxi. All ambushed by far-away bullets for unknown reasons.

I remember the scenes. I remember seeing detectives put on their bullet-proof vests so they wouldn't be the next victims. I remember the police asking our helicopter to search for clues from above.

Police knew the killings were connected, but they didn't know whether there was one or more shooters and they couldn't determine a motive from what appeared to be random targets. The police suspected, though, that the killers were in a white panel truck based upon reports by eyewitnesses who reported seeing such a truck near the shootings. Investigators believed the truck was the shooting platform the killers used. A federal/local task force was formed. Criminal profilers were engaged. There were lookouts for a white panel truck.

The white panel truck clue was helpful, but hundreds of businesses use white panel trucks. Put this to the test: Go to a nearby shopping center; close your eyes; open them; look quickly around. Chances are, you will see one and probably more than one white panel truck.

After each shooting, cops would choke off the scene, block traffic every which way, and search every vehicle. Vehicles were backed up for miles. But they found no killers.

We soon learned one thing: The shooters watched the news. When we reported that all the shootings were in Maryland, they shot people in Virginia. When we reported that all the shootings were in daylight, they shot people at night. When we reported that no children been shot, they shot a child going to school.

I received calls about new shootings at all hours of the day and night, and with a crew I would race to the crime scenes, go live on TV, and report details of the latest murder. For the most part, it was a study in fear and frustration.

Everyone was on high alert. Everyone hoped that he or she would not be the next victim.

Ultimately, the snipers' egos did them in. At one shooting scene they left a Tarot card—the death card. On it they had written the message: "Call me God. For you Mr. Police. Code: Call me God. Do not release to the press."

At other shooting scenes they left letters and ransom demands. At one scene the snipers left a bone-chilling threat: "Your children are not safe anywhere anytime."

It felt as though the snipers were toying with law enforcement and the public. They demanded that Montgomery County Police Chief Charles Moose read a crazy riddle on television. He did – on live TV: "You have asked us to say we have caught the sniper like a duck in a noose. I understand that hearing us say that is important to you." To this day, I have no clue as to what that meant. The riddle, though, gives you some idea of the kind of control the snipers exerted over the investigators and the whole Washington area.

Law enforcement finally got a break: the fingerprint on the Tarot death card was that of Lee Boyd Malvo. A background check of Malvo showed a link to John Allen Muhammad, which led them to a

New Jersey tag on a 1990 blue Chevy Caprice. After reviewing police reports, investigators discovered that a blue Chevy Caprice had also been sighted near some of the sniper scenes.

With the fingerprint, the tag, and the car description investigators had more than just a theory. On October 24, 2002, acting on a tip from a truck driver, the police found Malvo and Muhammad asleep in the blue Chevy alongside Interstate 70 in Myersville, Maryland. Everyone in the region breathed a collective sigh of relief. The nightmare was over. Life returned to normal.

The span of Muhammad's and Malvo's crimes extended from February 16 to October 23, 2002. During their three-week shooting rampage in the District, Virginia, and Maryland, Muhammad and Malvo killed ten and wounded another three people. There were seventeen victims in other jurisdictions.

John Allen Muhammad was born John Allen Williams in Baton Rouge, Louisiana in 1960. His maternal grandmother and an aunt raised him after his mother died when he was three. Williams enlisted in the Louisiana Army National Guard as a combat engineer and later transferred to the Regular Army. He served in the first Gulf War with a company that dismantled Iraqi chemical warfare rockets. While he was in the military, Williams was trained as a mechanic, a truck driver, and a specialist metalworker and became an expert marksman, earning the Expert Rifleman's Badge. After having served 17 years in the Army, Williams was honorably discharged from the Army in 1994. While Williams was in the military, he joined the Nation of Islam. In 2001 he changed his surname to Muhammad.   He was twice divorced; Muhammad's second wife sought and was granted a restraining order against him, which was outstanding at the time of the shootings.

Lee Boyd Malvo was 17 at the time of the shootings.   He was born in Jamaica to parents who later divorced. When he was 14, he was baptized into the Seventh Day Adventist Church; he attended a Seventh Day Adventist School, where he received good grades.

In 1999, Malvo moved to Antigua to join his mother. There he met Muhammad who was one of his mother's friends. Malvo's mother left her son in Muhammad's care when she emigrated illegally to the U.S. He converted Malvo to Islam. Malvo emigrated illegally to the U.S. in 2001, was arrested by Border Police, and was released on bail. He then traveled to Washington State, where he stayed with Muhammad in a homeless shelter near Takoma. While in Washington, Malvo shoplifted a Bushmaster XM-15 from the Bull's Eye Shooter Supply and practiced on the range adjacent to the gun shop.

Under federal law, neither Malvo nor Muhammad was allowed to possess a gun, Malvo because he was illegal and Muhammad because of the outstanding restraining order.

Muhammad groomed Malvo for the assaults, working him out, refining his shooting skills, and even controlling the young man's diet. Using skills he learned in the military, Muhammad rigged the blue Chevy Caprice so that Malvo could lie on his belly in the trunk and fire shots out of a hole in the trunk lid. The Caprice, was, in its prior life, a police car.

Some investigators believed that Muhammad's motive might have been the murder of his ex-wife who lived in the Washington area – that he planned to kill her and make it appear as though she were just another of the snipers' random targets.

Muhammad was convicted of capital murder in Virginia in 2003 and was sentenced to death. While awaiting execution he was extradited to Maryland, where he was convicted of six counts of first-degree murder on May 30, 2006. He was returned to Virginia after his Maryland conviction and executed on November 10, 2009. Appeals for trials in other jurisdictions remained pending at the time of his death.

Malvo was tried in Virginia in 2003 for two capital crimes of murder. While he was jailed pending trial, Malvo made a recorded confession to Detective Samuel Walker in which he stated that he "intended to kill them all." At the trial's beginning, Malvo pleaded not guilty by reason of insanity, claiming that he was under Muhammad's complete control. The court rejected his plea, and the trial proceeded.

During the trial, Malvo admitted that he had trained by shooting a real gun at paper plates that represented human heads. One of his defense attorneys said that violent video games had desensitized Malvo and contributed significantly to Malvo's state of mind and his willingness to commit murder. On December 3, 2003, Malvo was found guilty on both murder charges, and in March, 2004, he was sentenced to life without parole. In October of that year, he pleaded guilty to additional charges in Virginia and was given an additional life sentence without parole. He is serving his life sentences at the Red Onion State Prison in Virginia.

JR, THE HILLBILLY HITMAN

Fair warning this is a complicated story you may have to read it twice. But I think it's worth it. So here goes.

It was literally a case of "who struck John"—a perfectly planned and executed murder. Almost.

June 10, 1993. John Kowalczyk, a Virginia real estate developer, was shot in the head as he sat in a truck outside an office building in Vienna, Virginia. It happened around eight o'clock in the evening. He was 38 years old.

Kowalczyk had just spent some time with his 12-year-old son, Nicholas. He was waiting to hand the boy off to his ex-wife Katherine. It was a pre-arranged exchange. Nicholas got out of the car to put some trash in a nearby dumpster when—

Bam!

One shot did it. A 30-caliber round struck Kowalczyk in the head. He slumped down in his seat.

Kowalczyk was shot about a mile away from the Vienna, Virginia, police department. In minutes, cops were on the scene. For Vienna, this was a big deal. Murder was a stranger in Vienna, a Beaver Cleaver community that was home to many retired military and CIA agents. Breaking-and-entering was a major offense in Vienna; murder was unheard of. The chief himself was called in for this one.

TV: People Who Make the News You See

John Kowalczyk was no random victim—this was a hit, plain and simple, and the shooter knew what he was doing. The gunman used something called a sabot, a plastic sleeve that slips over the bullet, a device that makes it difficult to match ballistics.

To follow this case you need a scorecard and a map.

John Kowalczyk was something less than Man of the Year. He was known as a ruthless developer. He made a lot of money in the '80s and lost most of it in the '90s; creditors were hot on his trail.

Find a debt, find a motive.

When it came to love, Kowalczyk lived a soap-opera life. In 1979, he married Katherine Hyman, the daughter of Stanley and Jacqueline Hyman. The Kowalczyk's had two boys, Nicholas and Michael. But there was trouble in paradise.

John Kowalczyk fell in love with Lisa Zumwalt, who was married to James Zumwalt, son of Admiral Elmo Zumwalt. James Zumwalt, an attorney, was furious. He had a number of face-to-face fights with Kowalczyk. At one-point Zumwalt sent a woman "investigator" to romance Kowalczyk and had a private eye photograph the two making out. Zumwalt showed those make-out pictures to his wife in an effort to win her back, but Lisa Zumwalt wasn't impressed.

Find the spurned lover, find the suspect. Shortly after the investigation zeroed in on Zumwalt, he suffered a near-fatal overdose.

Stanley Hyman, Katherine Kowalczyk's father, was a retired Air Force colonel. He made a living counseling military people transitioning into civilian life. Stanley Hyman had paid a substantial sum to finance his daughter's divorce from Kowalczyk. Hyman also supported his daughter and her children because, when it came to monthly child support, Kowalczyk usually came up short. When police talked to Kowalczyk's 12year-old son Nicholas on the night of the murder, he blurted out something like, "They didn't have to kill him, just put him in jail for not paying child support."

Find the hurt, find the motive.

One other thing: Stanley Hyman was what you might call a gun enthusiast. The basement of his McLean home contained a firing range. He had an extensive gun collection. He had one other thing: an alibi. On the night of the Kowalczyk murder, Stanley and his wife were conducting one of their career-counseling clinics. Fifty people could vouch for that.

More than vengeance might have been involved. There was a matter of money. John Kowalczyk had taken out substantial life-insurance policies on himself which named his two children as beneficiaries. Katherine, his ex-wife, had custody of the children, who were minors; if John died while the children were still minors, she would have control of the insurance proceeds. There were no insurance proceeds, though. Being strapped for cash, Kowalczyk had cashed in both of the policies. Few people knew that.

The cops had some good leads but little hard evidence. What made it even more frustrating was the cooperation—not that they weren't getting any—they were almost getting too much. Kowalczyk's creditors gave the police a lot of information. James Zumwalt had candid conversations with them. The Hymans talked and gave the police tours of the firing range. They even disclosed that Colonel Hyman owned a Thompson Contender, the type of gun that killed Kowalczyk. Everybody was so nice – too nice.

Weeks went by. There was a lot of smoke but no fire.

Then one day a sheriff's office in West Virginia received a call that an ex-con and junkie named James Alting was missing. Sergeant Mark Cowles went to Alting's house to investigate, where he found a a slip of paper in James' room. It turned out to be one of the key clues in the case of the Hillbilly Hitman.

James Alting had done time up north and moved in with his parents when he was released from jail. Robert Alting and his wife lived in a white bungalow just up the hill from the famous hot baths in Berkeley Springs, West Virginia. James lived upstairs.

James Alting was last seen by his parents on the morning of June 19, 1993. They told the police they heard a car pull up to their house that evening and a car door open and close. They figured it was James' old 1976 Buick, but he didn't come inside. The next morning they found the car parked on the street— unusual, they said, because James always parked his car in the driveway.

James worked as a groundskeeper at Coolfont, a resort in the Berkeley Springs mountains. Coolfont was a West Virginia-style Walden—a place where people went to quit smoking, get massages, and think great thoughts.

For James Alting, Coolfont was a place to push dirt, pick up a paycheck, and keep the parole officer off his back. He had no reason to run. He had no reason to stay. He wasn't from Berkeley Springs—he wasn't one of them. If you're not one of them and all of sudden you vanish, well, it's not likely anybody's going to rush outside and turn on the air-raid siren.

James Alting's disappearance was John Ketterman's very first out-of-the-box case as a brand-new deputy-sheriff investigator. A former DC police detective, Ketterman was from West Virginia. Even though he'd spent years working big-city streets, Ketterman's demeanor was that of a country cop. He had a boyish face, wore off-the-rack suits, and listened a lot more than he talked.

Ketterman lived by three commandments:

- Never stand in front of a door when you knock.
- Always watch people's hands.
- If you're talking to a suspect and he follows you out the door telling his side of the story, chances are he's lying.

July 12, 1993, was John Ketterman's first day on the job as chief detective for the Morgan County sheriff's office. It was about one month after that murder in Vienna .On his first day as Ketterman walked into the office, there on a wooden chair was a beefy man with a shaved head and a beard. He looked like a professional wrestler. His name was Ralph Shambaugh, Jr., but everybody called him JR. His daddy was the Morgan County clerk. JR worked as a bouncer at a number of bars and, at times, was among their best customers. He also worked as a maintenance man at the Coolfont Resort. JR was at the sheriff's office because he had been charged with malicious wounding. He didn't stay locked up long Perhaps because Berkeley Springs is a small town and JR's daddy was the County Clerk.

On Ketterman's first day at the sheriff's office he was dispatched to the Robert Alting's house to take a missing persons report .

Robert Alting and his wife had moved to Berkeley Springs to spend his retirement years in peace and quiet. They didn't have much of either. Mr. Alting's wife was disabled and hooked up to oxygen. Their son, a junkie out of prison for a short time, was missing.

This did not appear to be a Perry Mason mystery. You could make a case that the dark side got the better of James Alting and he simply ran away except for one thing: his car. Why would a man on the run leave his car in front of the family home?

John Ketterman went to Robert Alting's house. He looked at James' car. Mr. Alting took him up to his son's room. "I was impressed by how neat that room was," Ketterman said. " Everything just so." Ketterman noticed a matchbook on James' dresser. It was from the Vienna Wolf Trap Inn. When Ketterman asked Mr. Alting about his son's friends, Mr. Alting said his son hung out with a guy known as JR.

Later that day, Ketterman compared notes with Sergeant Cowles who said there was a name and two telephone numbers on the slip of paper he had found in James' room. The name was Highman [sic] and the phone numbers were from Virginia. Cowles called one of the numbers. A man answered. He identified himself as Stanley Hyman. Cowles asked Hyman "How would you know a man like James Alting?" to which Hyman replied "I go to Coolfont a lot. I deal in guns. Maybe I talked to him about guns."

It gets even better. As it turns out, Stanley Hyman and his wife were at Coolfont the weekend James Alting disappeared. They had left abruptly. Hyman said they left because he was attacked outside his cabin and was so shaken by the experience that he drove back to his home in McLean to see a doctor. He said he was so distraught he didn't report the attack until he arrived in Virginia.

Hyman's story stunk.

Detective Ketterman went to Coolfont. People there didn't think much of Hyman's story, either. Coolfont Resort didn't have roads; it had trails. The only things that attacked people outside their cabins were mosquitoes. The people at Coolfont told Ketterman something that turned out to be important: JR Shambaugh was James Alting's supervisor.

Although Ketterman now worked in West Virginia, he watched Washington news. He knew about the Kowalczyk murder, and he knew about Hyman.

Ketterman called the Vienna, Virginia police. He said" I asked them if their Hyman might be my Highman. We compared phone numbers, and they matched. It was time for a road trip. I went to the sheriff and said this had potential to be a really big case I don't think he believed me, but he let me go to Vienna anyway to check it out."

With two Vienna detectives, Ketterman went to the Wolf Trap Inn, an old-style motel about a mile from the murder scene. It looked like a place some people might rent by the day and use by the hour. There was no lobby – just a tiny office. Guests would go in, pay, and head off to one of the metal-doored rooms with little slivers of soap. Ketterman and the detectives walked into the front office. Ketterman asked the clerk "Did you have a James Alting registered here around June 10th?"

"No, "said the clerk.

Ketterman began to sweat. He thought he had solved the case: Angry ex-in-laws hired an ex-con to knock off the ex-husband; the in-laws' phone numbers found in ex-con's room; the ex-con on the loose, his getaway car left behind. Case Closed. When the clerk said Alting had not been a registered guest, Ketterman saw his theory melt away. As the Vienna detectives and Ketterman prepared to leave, in sort of a Columbo-type moment, Ketterman asked, "Did you ever have a JR Shambaugh registered here?" The clerk scanned the files again. "Yes" he said. "He was here."

BALLGAME!

Ketterman was ready to get a warrant. Bob Horan had other ideas.

Bob Horan was a red-faced, rumpled-suit, fighting-Irish lawyer who, for nearly four decades, had been the chief prosecutor for Fairfax County, Virginia. Bob Horan had a reputation: he sent bad guys away. If you were a criminal, Bob Horan would be the last man you wanted to see. He hit the long ball; he rarely lost a big case. In court he would fight like a pit bull, grab onto the facts, get up-close and personal with the jurors—

and before it was over, Bob Horan would get a conviction.

Horan made the old adage "One picture is worth a thousand words" an integral part of his courtroom strategy. During his closing arguments in murder cases, Horan would drape crime-scene photos on the railing in front of the jurors—and leave them there. When the defense attorneys got up to make their case, they found the jurors staring right at pictures of the slaughtered victims.

When a big case came along, Bob Horan would take charge, not just of the trial but of the entire investigation. It's like Horan was baking a cake: he knew the ingredients he needed, and he didn't stop collecting and mixing them until he knew that everything would come out just right when things were done.

Horan met with the investigators in the Kowalczyk murder case and warned them that there was a big difference between a theory and evidence, and that they didn't have diddly squat.

That was soon to change.

After Ketterman returned to West Virginia he got a call from someone at the Coolfont resort. "I need to talk," the man said. "I think someone is out to kill me." Ketterman met a man he called S in the man's mobile home. The man was nervous and went around closing the shades. He told Ketterman he often hung out and went drinking with JR Shambaugh and Alting. S asked Ketterman "What do you want to know?" Ketterman replied "Everything."

S then told this story: Weeks before, JR had showed him a picture of John Kowalczyk and told him, "We got people who want me to take this guy out." JR offered $5,000 to S to drive. S told JR he would think it over but said he never got back to JR. He said that after the murder, he saw Kowalczyk's picture in the paper, and it didn't take long for him to figure out who had murdered him. He knew Alting was missing, and he figured that was JR's doing, too. When S questioned JR about Kowalczyk's death, JR told him he decided not to do it.

S knew he was the one person who could finger JR, and he knew that if JR had killed once, maybe twice, it wouldn't take much for him to do it a third time. S told Ketterman "Unless you guarantee protection I'm not going to give it up." Arrangements were made to move S out of state.

This was one of the biggest cases Vienna police had ever handled—so big the chief himself showed up at the murder scene, which turned out to be fortuitous. When the detectives told the chief about JR and gave a rough description of him, the chief said he remembered seeing someone like that at the scene *after* the murder. Could it be that JR had stayed around to admire his handiwork?

The detectives decided to handle the chief like a witness. They prepared a photo spread with pictures of JR and several other men. They arranged them like playing cards on a table. The chief didn't hesitate; he reached for JR's photo.

The police went all out to investigate JR. They knew he paid cash at the Wolf Trap Inn. When it came to phone calls, though, he was Mr. Credit. On the night John Kowalczyk was murdered, a number of calls were charged to JR's phone card – calls made to Stanley Hyman's McLean home.

The police found that, before the murder, JR deposited $9,000 in cash in a Berkeley Spring bank; bought a special night-vision device; and took some family and friends to Ocean City, where he went on a spending spree. They hopped from bar to bar; JR picked up all the tabs. Not bad for a maintenance man at a mountain retreat.

Now Horan was starting to get the ingredients he needed. It was grand-jury time.

Stanley and Jacqueline Hyman were nervous, so nervous that they hit the road. They told friends they were just going away for a little vacation. On July 22, they rented a condo in Clearwater, Florida. On July 27, they went to Bill Jackson's Sporting Goods in Pinellas Park, Florida and purchased a 12-gauge shotgun and some shells. The bill: $164.73.

On August 4, their son Michael called the Clearwater condo. No answer. He tried again. Nothing. Michael called the management office, which sent a security guard to the Hyman's condo. There he found them – dead.

Stanley Hyman was in his underwear, the shotgun beneath his feet. Both had fatal gunshot wounds to the head. Police believe Jacqueline Hyman knelt down and that her husband shot her in the forehead. They also believe that Stanley Hyman, concerned that blood had splattered on a nearby window, then pinned the curtains across the window and shot himself. On the dining room table detectives found eight or nine different notes. They were written in two different colors of ink and in two different handwriting styles. They were initialed and signed by Stanley and Jacqueline Hyman.

In the pile was a letter addressed to the Vienna police from Stanley Hyman: "Although all circumstantial evidence points to me and my family, we were not involved. The shooter may have been an idiot, but the individual who planned the murder obviously did his homework and was a long way from being a dummy."

Were the Hymans calling JR an idiot? On September 20, a grand jury indicted JR Shambaugh on first-degree murder charges in the shooting death of John Kowalczyk. It was one of the worst-kept secrets around. JR knew it was coming. His father knew it was coming. The gossips in Morgan County knew it was coming. JR was arrested and locked up weeks before the grand jury voted to indict him.

For Detective Ketterman, though, there was a loose end. Where was James Alting? Horan was interested, too, because with Alting still missing, JR could claim that Alting murdered Kowalczyk.

On June 13, 1994, one year and three days after John Kowalczyk's murder and before JR's trial, James Alting's body was found by JR's relatives in an abandoned well at a campground located on land owned by the Shambaugh family. Alting had been shot in the head.

JR Shambaugh's murder case ended in a mistrial, but in March,1995, JR pleaded guilty to accessory to murder and was sentenced to 35 years in prison. He was eligible for parole in 2002. His parole was revoked after he was arrested and jailed on a domestic assault charge. JR's new parole date is some time in 2024.

James Alting's death was ruled a homicide so far, no one charged in that case of murder.

K.C. Bohrer, a West Virginia law enforcement officer for over forty years, is now the Morgan County, West Virginia's Sheriff. Sheriff Bohrer says JR remains a person of interest in several homicides. Stay tuned.

7

TV: PEOPLE WHO MAKE
THE NEWS YOU SEE

BRENNER

When the fire alarm went off in Glenn Brenner's house, his wife Suzi quickly gathered the kids and ran outside to safety. Glenn frantically searched around the house, found a picture of himself in a Phillies uniform, and then ran to safety.

When Glenn won an Emmy he had it temporarily installed as a hood ornament on his Lincoln Town Car.

When he was suspended for a day for showing what the boss thought was an insensitive video, he showed up the next day in a prison outfit.

Glenn Brenner took nothing seriously. He was the funniest man I have ever known—a tall man with a large head and elastic face that he could wrinkle and distort in a kaleidoscope of shapes that would make you double over in laughter. Glenn Brenner was from Philadelphia—all you had to do was listen to him to figure that out. He had the sharp tongue and sarcastic swagger unique to migrants from the City of Brotherly

Love. Brenner once pitched in the Phillies farm system. I asked him, "When the bases were loaded and the manager came to the mound, what did he say to you?"

"Throw strikes," the manager said.

"Oh, that's it," said Brenner. "Throw strikes—now I get it!"

After baseball, Brenner got into broadcasting, first in radio, then television. He worked briefly for a station in Philadelphia, where he was fired because they said he talked too fast. Imagine someone in Philadelphia thinking anyone could talk too fast.

Brenner caught the eye of Jim Snyder, the news director at Channel 9 in Washington, and was hired as a backup to the famous Warner Wolf. When Warner went on to work at ABC I told Brenner, "Hey, this could be your chance to replace Warner Wolf." "No, no," Brenner said. "I don't want to replace Warner Wolf. I want to replace the guy who replaces Warner Wolf." Brenner was prescient.

Snyder hired a guy named Mike Wolfe to replace Warner. Mike Wolfe wore Nik Nik shirts and gold chains, and every month he would call for some coach somewhere to be fired. Mike Wolfe was fired himself before he had a chance to buy a tie.

Brenner became the main man and was an instant hit. He got Sister Mary Louise, a nun at Visitation High School, to pick NFL winners. He launched the "Weenie of the Week" for sports mishaps and miscreants. And when the Weenie mobile came to DC, guess who got to drive it around. Brenner was funniest when the wheels came off and the scripts got lost and the prompter didn't work or the wrong tape rolled. He was the conductor of chaos. No matter what happened, Brenner would leave you laughing. He transcended sports—people who hated sports would tune in just to see what he was going to do.

If you thought Brenner was funny on the air, you should have gone to a bar with him. Brenner and his wife Suzi went to Chadwicks in Georgetown with my wife Emily and me. Motown was playing. Brenner loved Motown. He started to lead the crowd in song. Someone said, "No, Glenn, someone's going to recognize you." Brenner grabbed a Sharpie from a waitress and drew a mustache on his face." Better now?" he said.

Glenn was diagnosed with a brain tumor. We visited him in the hospital. It was during a WFT playoff run towards the Super Bowl. Late one night after a playoff game, in the dark halls of the hospital, we saw a figure walking towards Glenn's room. It was 'Skins coach Joe Gibbs. No entourage, just Joe Gibbs by himself. He brought Glenn the game ball.

On January 14, 1992, Glenn Brenner died; he was just 44 years old. After Glenn's death, the News at Channel 9 was never quite the same.

NEWSWOMEN

Some of the best newsmen I have encountered over the years have been women. Tough, relentless finders of facts, wordsmiths who can craft a story that makes you stop what you are doing and listen. These are just a few of the remarkable newswomen I have met along the way.

Cassie Mackin, Trailblazer

1972: Cassie Mackin was the first woman to report from the floor of political conventions.

1976: Cassie Mackin was the first woman to regularly anchor a network evening newscast.

Cassie Mackin experienced a meteoric rise from a reporter at the Baltimore News American in 1960 to the Hearst Washington bureau in 1963, WRC-TV in 1969, NBC in 1971, and ABC in 1977.

Cassie received numerous accolades, including Emmys, but I don't remember her for any of that.

In the early Sixties, when I was still in high school and just learning the art of reporting and writing, I was selected to cover the Student Youth Congress, a gathering of 102 high school students from all over the country that was funded by the Hearst Foundation. The Youth Congress afforded students an opportunity to meet their Congressmen and learn about government. I was supposed to provide readers with a teenager's view of the conference. It was my first journalistic road trip, and I was excited. Well, it wasn't exactly a road trip; I lived in DC and the Congress was at the Mayflower Hotel in DC, but I got to stay at the Mayflower so that I could cover the Congress wall-to-wall. I had a portable typewriter, stacks of paper, and a suitcase packed with clothes. I was ready.

Cassie Mackin mentored me during that project. With her career taking off, she could easily have given me short shrift and moved on to something more important, but she didn't. Each day, she checked just about every word in every story and told me how to improve it. She taught me how to tell the story of one so it would reflect the feeling of all. I wrote only a few stories over a few days, Cassie improved each one, teaching me, and encouraging me as she did so. Cassie Mackin was an important person in my young journalistic life.

Cassie died of cancer at age 42. All the kings and queens of television news went to her funeral. I said an Irish prayer for her.

Betty Endicott, Trailblazer

Betty Endicott moved to WDVM in Washington in 1980. By that time, she had been a reporter, a producer, an assignment editor, and an executive editor at multiple news organizations, but she had never been a news director. When Betty joined WDVM, she not only became a news director, she became Washington DC's first female news director. She was fond of saying that when she was made news director everyone could count the number of women who had held that job on one mitten.

In 1982 Betty left WDVM to become the assignment manager of Metro Media's national bureau. The following year she was named news director at the local Fox station. When she arrived at Fox, it had five reporters and three crews. By 1987, she oversaw nine full-time and two free lance reporters, six commentators, eight crews, and two microwave trucks with engineers, and she did it masterfully. Betty made a difference every place she worked.

Nancy Dickerson, another icon in the TV news business, told the Washington Post that Betty Endicott was simply a "feisty, gutsy female. . . ." Dickerson said Endicott's success was based on letting everyone do his own thing, letting reporters pursue stories even though she didn't always agree. She gave many young reporters a break in the business, including Brian Williams.

Endicott was not only a soccer mom, she played soccer. "Don't come near my goal," she would say, and that competitive spirit led to great success in the local TV business.

I never worked with Betty: she joined the Channel 9 team as I was leaving. That was my loss.

Andrea Mitchell

Andrea Mitchell, reporter for KYW radio and sister station KYW TV, had already covered Mayor Frank Rizzo as a Philadelphia radio reporter, a daunting, but exciting, task, when Jim Snyder, Channel 9 DC's news director, hired her to cover politics on Washington TV. One of Andrea's assignments was covering Marvin Mandel, the controversial and colorful governor of Maryland who succeeded Spiro Agnew when he became President Nixon's VP. In 1977 Mandel was convicted of mail fraud and racketeering for taking payoffs in a racetrack rigging scandal. At the time, Mandel and his wife, Bootsie, were going through an ugly divorce, and Mandel needed money. It was a real-life soap opera; Bootsie even kicked Mandel out of the governor's mansion. Andrea Mitchell was all over it.

Her excellent coverage of the comings and goings of Marvin Mandel caught the eye of the big shots at NBC network, and she was gone from Channel 9 News before we could say Nightly News.

For decades Andrea has been tracking politicians, their deeds and misdeeds. She has the best contact list in Washington. Who doesn't want to talk to Andrea? All the while she does this in a quiet and classy way, quick to share credit and kudos for her many scoops. Andrea Mitchell will leave a lasting mark in the world of television news.

Guess who picked up the Mandel story when Andrea left for a bigger, greener pasture?

Kris Ostrowski

If it weren't for television news, there's a good chance Brett Marcus and Kris Ostrowski might never have met.

Brett Marcus was, among other things, an urbane New Yorker, a fancy dresser, and a gourmet. He might have seemed "high-browed," but he was very much everyman's kind of guy.

Kris Ostrowski was a California woman with Midwest values. She was quick-thinking and hard charging. She was never accused of using dainty words.

The team of Marcus and Ostrowski ruled Channel 4 News in the Eighties and led the station to a solid number-one in virtually every newscast. Brett had a knack for identifying stories that had legs, stories with consequences that hit home with the people in and around Washington. Kris had a no-nonsense way of marshaling reporters and crews to get those stories on the air. They did it better than anyone else. Through the Marion Barry years, through blizzards, through all sorts of city ups and downs, they were a top-notch team.

Alas, teams, great or not, don't last forever. Brett moved on. Kris became news director; though she was masterful at managing down, she was not masterful at "managing up." There are consequences to telling your boss to shove it.

Margie Ruttenberg

Take a close look at TV reporters and you will notice that each of them has a small device in his ear. It is called an IFB. I think it means interrupt frequency broadcast. The device allows producers and directors to talk into a reporter's ear while he is live on television. This can either be helpful or it can be distracting. Margie Ruttenberg had one of the most soothing voices I have ever heard in my ear.

From 1990 until 2008 Margie worked at NBC4. Most of that time she was a producer. Much of that time she coordinated some of the DC metro area's most important stories. Margie was working on 9/11 when Charlie Bragale yelled that a plane was flying too low near the Pentagon. She ran to the control room. From the control room she steered stories about the snipers whose random killings caused the entire metro region to panic. Margie was a calming presence in the control room, steering both big and small news stories.

What Margie remembers most, though, was an encounter she had while on jury duty. One day, while on her way home, she saw a group of young black men near a subway stop literally singing for their supper. They called themselves "Just Us." She was impressed by their sound and dedication, returned to the station, and arranged for Vance to do a story on the group. A music producer took notice and "Just Us" was off to the Apollo.

Soon after Margie was diagnosed with blood cancer, she left the TV business. But she has never left our hearts.

Catherine Snyder

I call her Mother Superior.

In the News business we have a line beyond which we don't tread, but as mores, rules, and the definitions of words change, the line moves. For a reporter to end up on the wrong side of the line can have dire consequences. Can you say this word on television? Can you show this picture? Are these facts or just a pile of rumors? Want to stay on the right side of the line? Ask Mother Superior. Mother knows best.

The news business is in Catherine Snyder's DNA. You see, you can't talk about Catherine without mentioning Big Jim – Jim Snyder, her dad who put together a news team that was dominant in Washington for many years. At the Snyder home, young Catherine would watch her dad as he surveyed all the newscasts and rated the reporters he saw on TV.

Sometimes Catherine would act as a human TV remote control.

In the newsroom Big Jim read every word of every script of everything said on television. Catherine became a top newswoman by reading every word of every script.

It was Big Jim's way.
It's Catherine's way.
It's the Snyder way.
It's the right way.

Ede Jermin

When you see coverage of a Stanley Cup victory parade, Ede Jermin is behind the scenes

If there's coverage of an Inauguration or a political convention, Ede Jermin makes it happen.

If there is a big trial or a storm with a name attached, Ede Jermin finds a way to get it on TV.

News stories don't appear on your television screen by magic. The airing of the news requires planning, logistics, credentials, crew deployment— everything from satellite time to sandwiches. It requires a great deal of coordination. One little glitch could mean disaster and the end of someone's news career.

For years Ede has coordinated the coverage of big stories for News4. For the most part, it's a thankless job. When things go well, few people give Ede a high five, but if something goes sideways, it's watch out. She orchestrates big-time TV coverage with the precision of a field marshal while maintaining her concern for the needs and feelings of the people who do the job.

In 2009, there were some sad times. GE, NBC's owner, prepared to sell NBC and other assets. It trimmed staff – more than two dozen people from our newsroom. Ede helped organize a party to celebrate the contributions of the departing employees. A manager told her not to get involved, but Ede did it anyway. That day Ede was out front and it made a difference.

Heather Hutchinson

When they bury Heather Hutchinson, they had better bury her tripod alongside her. She carries the damn thing with her everywhere – up and down stairs, up and down hills, down alleys – her cameras slung over her shoulders, her tripod cradled in her arms, both always at the ready. You see, Heather demands every shot she takes to be sharp, and that requires her camera to be rock solid. Enter her trusty tripod.

Heather has rules – her rules – and she doesn't break her rules. One of her rules is always carry a fanny pack with a lavaliere mike and extra batteries. Another is never let the live truck appear in the shot. No matter how rushed we might be, how little time we have to get on the air, Heather Hutchinson never breaks the rules.

I have been lucky that, for most of my time in television, I have been paired with the same cameraman for chunks of time. It has made a big difference. It's like having the same dance partner. The cameraman knows me, what I am likely to do and say, and how I'm likely to move. I've worked with first-class cameramen: Jay Alvey, then Dan Buckley, Luis Urbina, SeanCasey, Jim Kizer, and now Heather Hutchinson.

For more than eight years, Heather and I have traveled about the DC Metro area in a TV live truck, Heather at the wheel. She drives the truck; she shoots the stories; she edits the stories; she puts in the live shots; she shoots the live shots; and when it's all over she breaks it all down. Heather is engaged in the stories. She tracks down leads, talks to witnesses at the scene, and finds ways to advance the story, and moves the ball down the field towards the goal. Over the years Heather and I have had our share of arguments—but the story always wins.

THE ART AND SCIENCE OF TELEVISION NEWS

Since the beginning of time art and science have been at war. Artists believe they have the key to the human soul. Scientists believe they have the ability to discover and formulate the truth of life. The war is never-ending. Articles are

Crime reporting at Channel 9

written, documentaries are made—on and on and on.

Some people believe TV news is an art; others want to make it a science. Send in the consultants. Many news consultants believe they have an empirical formula for success that crosses boundaries. They believe that stations which implement the magic formula will – presto! – achieve overnight success.

Usually the formula involves short stories, high story counts, bold graphics, hard-driving music, end-of-the-world urgency, and having someone on the air say, "Breaking News," every two minutes. I believe there are some producers who get bonuses each time someone says, "Breaking news." To be fair it's not always "Breaking news"—sometimes it's "Developing Story." It's an electronic way of grabbing someone by the collar and saying, "Watch this—don't you dare change the channel."

Whether you like it or not, let's move on to the weather. For many television stations, weather centers have become "storm centers." People don't just want to know about the weather, they want to know about dangerous weather—impending doom, wire-snapping winds, crippling snow, flood waters. There are alerts with dramatic graphics that change from soothing shades of blue to stop-sign red.

You get the idea. Create a sense of urgency, of drama.

Consultants tell news organizations that what they need is an anchor who can sit on the edge of a chair, look into the camera, and, with a great sense of urgency, deliver rapid-fire stories oneafteranother-afteranother. I am breathless just thinking about it. Now, get in your SUV, travel the country, and sell this snake oil to general managers and news directors far and wide. Before you know it, the entire nation – the world – will be watching those news shows and becoming more engaged and excited with every graphic change.

Or not.

Whoops! I forgot one important ingredient: RESEARCH. News organizations spend tons of money doing surveys to find out what kind of news viewers want to see on television. Still there is no guarantee that what is broadcast is what viewers want to see and hear. Most surveys are flawed for two reasons.

Reason number one: People don't always respond honestly in surveys. "I want to see more good news," they say. Really? "Plane lands safely at National Airport." "High-school graduates students who can read and write." "Your tap water is safe to drink." Fill a newscast with those kinds of stories, and the broadcast of the Mass for shut-ins will have more viewers. NORMALCY IS NOT NEWS.

The saying is that if you eat steak and the only steak you ever eat is Swiss steak, you'll never know what a New York strip tastes like. The reporter's job is to go out into the highways and byways and find life's New York strips and then bring that bacon home—boy, did I mix that metaphor—but you get the idea.

THE ART OF TV NEWS

A little-talked-about television secret: most of the time, EVERYBODY HAS THE SAME STORIES. What makes one station different from the next is the ability to tell the story in a compelling and meaningful way. Television news is a personal business, a visceral business. If you do a good job telling a story, it should hit home touch your heart—make you sad, make you angry, make you smile. The ability to look down the barrel of a camera lens and tell a story that has impact is a powerful gift. That's what makes one news show better than the next. And if you get a stable of storytellers together, you'll have a winner. And everybody will be eating New York strips.

EARLY LOCAL NEWS

In the early years of television, news was an afterthought, a public service. Stations presented news to keep their broadcast licenses. The newscasts could be 15 minutes or half an hour, usually with a guy in a velvet blazer reading wire copy with a couple slides: a ball score and a brief weather report. Bingo, bango, bongo—that's the news, we did it, now let's move on. No "Hey, Helen, look at this!" moments. If people really wanted news they read newspapers or listened to the radio. Television news was a novelty. People watched television to be entertained: nationally – Howdy Doody, Sid Caesar, Ed Sullivan and locally – Ranger Hal, Pick Temple, Bowling for Dollars.

My whole family used to sit around a gigantic piece of furniture with a tiny black-and-white screen in the middle – all quiet in the room – waiting for the next act on Ed Sullivan. It was exciting. Why, it was almost like being at the movies. Indeed, I think my baby boomer generation was the first to grow up with TV.

The early televisions had big tubes that took a long time to warm up and fuzzy black-and-white pictures. Then came not-so-colorful color pictures and Winky Dink and You. Every year there were new programs at new times, something to look forward to. Television went from the living room to the TV room. At breakfast we would ask, "What's on tonight?"

As television became more and more a part of our lives, television executives made a valuable discovery: LOCAL NEWS CAN MAKE MONEY. They just had to figure a way to do it. Out went the velvet jackets and the primitive slides. In came the film crews, reporters, writers, and a new brand of anchors.

There were some misfires. Channel 9 in Washington had something called The Big News. It was anchored by Tom Braden and Martin Agronsky. Tom Braden was a former CIA official, the author of Eight Is Enough, and a Washington mover and shaker. Martin Agronsky was an accomplished reporter, a war correspondent, and a political expert. It was an authoritative team that provided few "Hey, Helen," moments.

In the early years of local news, the teleprompters were long scrolls of paper, mounted below the camera lens, that would be rolled along so the anchor could read and read and read, as if he had memorized the news of the day. Those words and phrases were typed onto the scrolls with a gigantic typewriter by a production assistant well in advance of show time. Which gets me to a story I'm reluctant to tell. Reluctant because I am not totally sure it is true. It may be just a fable but here goes.

Martin Agronsky was said to be somewhat irritable at times, sometimes less than gentle to the "little people" who worked on his show. Included among the little people was the production assistant responsible for typing and rolling that prompter for the newscast. Martin Agronsky had a signature signoff. A lot of anchors did (and do):

Edward R. Murrow : "Good night and Good Luck"

Walter Cronkite: "And that's the way it is."

Tim Russert: " If it's Sunday, it's Meet the Press."

Dave Garroway: "Peace."

Dan Rather: "Courage."

Ron Burgundy: "You stay classy, San Diego."

For Martin Agronsky it was "That's the big news. I'm Martin Agronsky." Martin Agronsky was married to the teleprompter; if it was on the prompter, Martin would say it.

One day the production assistant had had enough, and at the end of the script he wrote," And that's the big news. I'm Peter Rabbit." I don't think I need to finish the story. I don't know who that production assistant was or what happened to him, but I hope somewhere he is running a TV station—or a rabbit farm, or something fun. Truth or fable, the story shows how important the so-called "little people" can be to television news shows.

LOCAL NEWS DIRECTORS

Schools are judged by the success of their graduates. News directors are judged by the success of the people they hire. And, of course, ratings. There was a time when being a news director was a big deal—field-grade officer. Newsrooms, and for that matter, newscasts, often reflected the personality of the news director. He—and in some cases, she—had serious power. General managers had other things to worry them: sales, production, engineering, *et cetera*. But as stations produced more and more newscasts and did less and less TV production work, general managers got more and more involved in the day-to-day operations of the newsroom.

When I started back in 1973, we did around 15 minutes of news in the morning, a half hour at noon, an hour-and-a-half in the early evening, and a half hour late in the evening. The total time that was devoted to daily local news was two hours, forty-five minutes. Today it's three hours in the morning, an hour midday, three hours early evening, and a half hour late in the evening. The total time we devote to daily local news is seven-and-a-half hours. Local news determines the identity of the whole station. There is a lot of money at stake. General managers know that all too well.

I have worked for no fewer than 18 different news directors in my 46 years. Do the math: That's a new news director about every 2.9 years. There were times news directors were an endangered species.

My first—and best—news director was Jim Snyder. Jim had a radio background at Westinghouse and CBS. In fact, he was the news director at WTOP radio right before he came to run Channel 9.

We called Jim the "Lefty Driesell of local television." He was a great recruiter but something less than a gentle coach. Look at some of his hires: Gordon

Peterson, first TV job, Warner Wolf, first TV job, Andrea Mitchell, first TV job.

Snyder thought it was important to bring original reporting to local news. He thought it was better to teach reporters television than to try and teach broadcasters how to be reporters.

Every day Snyder read every word of every script for every news show. There were no morning staff meetings. First thing in the

Jim Snyder, News Director at Channel 9, put together a powerhouse team that dominated in DC for years

morning Snyder read the newspaper and caught up on the news. He would call the desk, dictate the assignments, and later make any needed adjustments. He was a tough taskmaster. It didn't take long for Channel 9 to become dominant in the ratings. We had anchors Gordon Peterson and Max Robinson; sports reporter Warner Wolf; weather reporter Louie Allen; and news reporters Mike Buchanan, Andrea Mitchell, Bruce Johnson, Steve Gendel, Susan King, and Henry Tenenbaum. In many cases our second team was stronger than the other stations' starters.

Snyder brought in Maureen Bunyan to replace Max when he went to the network; neither Bunyan, nor Snyder, nor the Station missed a beat. When Warner left, Snyder replaced him with Glenn Brenner.

When Louie Allen passed, Snyder replaced him with Gordon Barnes. The hits just kept on coming.

Then the unthinkable happened: THE SWAP

WTOP's owner, the Washington Post, traded Channel 9 to the Detroit News in exchange for a Detroit TV station. Why? The Post thought the Nixon government was going to prevent big-time papers from owning TV stations serving the same metro area. Before any law was passed or rule adopted to achieve such a goal, the Post did the swap with the Detroit News. The government didn't enact any law or propose any regulation that would have prevented the Post from continuing to own Channel 9, but it didn't matter for us—the swap was a done deal.

After the swap, Snyder left Channel 9.

I can remember only two times in my four-decades-plus of television that a station's staff has held a party for a news director (and paid for it themselves). Once was for Jim Snyder. As tough as Snyder was, everybody from anchors down to the couriers loved him. Jim had a tremendous impact on local news in Washington. There was a feeling that Channel 9 would not be the same after Jim's departure. It was more than just a feeling.

LOOK FOR THE UNION LABEL

Not long after the Detroit Evening News took over, anchor Gordon Peterson approached me and said there was a contract negotiation coming. He said he wanted to take his dear old dad to Ireland and asked if I would sit in on the negotiation for him.

There were two unions at the station, IBEW (International Brotherhood of Electrical Workers), representing the techs and field crews, and AFTRA (American Federation of Television and Radio Artists), representing the anchors, reporters, writers, and production assistants. Gordon was the AFTRA shop steward and union voice for the station.

The contract in question focused on the writers and production assistants. At the time, we had three writers and two production assistants, and though Channel 9 was number one in the market, the writers and production assistants were the lowest paid in the market. We tried to remedy that. At stake: about $25,000 over three years or about $5,000 per person. No problem right?

Oh, no—there was a problem.

The Detroit Evening News brought in a lawyer from Texas to negotiate on its behalf. He was a Franklin Mint version of a man. When he sat at the big conference table, his feet barely touched the ground. We talked and argued and talked and argued and then talked and argued some more. My God, you would have thought it was the Vietnam peace talks. All over 25 grand over three years for low-paid, behind-the-scenes workers. I think the Detroit Evening News was trying to make a point: There is a new sheriff in these here parts, and these are the new rules. There were whispers about a possible strike.

After days of back and forth, the little lawyer looked at me and said, "Collins, you can go out for ten minutes, ten days, or ten years—you're not going to get ten cents more." That was around three in the afternoon.

We were on strike two hours later.

We walked out. Scabs walked in. They patched together a newscast they figured people would watch because of the novelty of it all, but strangers stumbling through the television news was not a recipe for success. In less than four days, the strike was over, the $25,000 was agreed to, Gordon Peterson was back from the Emerald Isle, and everybody went back to work.

Now for the payback.

Everything was back to normal except—except when my contract came up for renewal, the Detroit Evening News had alligator arms. I think they offered me a raise of about $7.25, or something like that. Fortunately for me, three Chicago stations were interested in hiring me. There was a bidding war, and in the end I was off to the Windy City to work for WLS-TV, a fantastic ABC O&O (owned and operated), It was a sign from God.

It was also short-lived.

Chicago was, and is, a great no-bullshit news town, but it doesn't roll out the red carpet for outsiders. If you're not from She-caaa-go and you don't drink pop and you can't find Dee Von Street, the natives pick up on it right away. You might as well be from Russia. In those days I was a feature reporter. I was brought there to work on a new show. But WLS already had a talented and well-loved feature reporter, Frank Mathie, and when I walked in the door I got some cold shoulder and pretty hard eyeballs. In a short time, however, Frank and I became good friends, and I had a great time doing offbeat stories about the city with broad shoulders.

For my wife it was a different story. Emily came from a large Philadelphia family. Chicago was as far west as she had ever been. It was cold, and the Chicago area had things she had never seen before, like seiches (you know, those weird waves in a Great Lake). She was lonesome. In my job I met and made friends every day, but Emily was home with three children. For her the move was not easy, and I could be of little help when I wasn't at home. It's not like I could go to Sears and buy her a six-pack of friends. Emily called my agent almost daily to complain. She shed a lot of tears. When my three-year deal contract was done, it was back to DC.

INDOOR CATS AND OUTDOOR CATS

In the television news business, there are basically two kinds of workers—the managers, writers, producers, and editors who work inside the station, and the reporters and camera crews that work in the field. I say camera crews, but the truth is that in today's world it really is a camera man or woman working with the reporter. In some cases, the reporter shoots and edits his or her own story.

The field reporters and crews are journalistic gunslingers. They are like feral cats that roam the streets and alleys looking for stories. They try to persuade people who have witnessed or are caught up in a reportable event to talk. They encounter great sorrow and witness blood-stained murder scenes. On the streets, field crews get an unvarnished view of life's triumphs and tragedies; they have a front-row seat to the story of life. Field crews' lives on the street can be raw, stressful, and rewarding all at the same time.

The people inside a news station deal with stories from afar through phone calls and videos fed in from the field. They don't have a front-row seat to events happening outside the station. In the station there is no blood on the ground and no tear stains on your shirt. The insiders are the first viewers evaluating stories in an act of journalistic triage.

DRESSED TO TELL

Sometimes the best way to tell a story is from inside it. I learned that a long time ago in the sports department of the Washington Daily News.

Washington-Lee High School had a championship crew team that was so good that it earned a chance participate in the Henley Cup Regatta in England. The problem was getting there. The team didn't have money – at least not enough to go to England.

Back then, Washington was a one-team town and the team was the WFT. Crew was, at best, a sidebar sport. So, in an effort to shine some light on Washington-Lee, I spent a day with the school's crew team on the Potomac. In a single day, I learned how to board the paper-thin shell of a boat, how to handle an oar, the importance of synchronized stroking, and the pain of catching a crab when an oar socks you in your jaw.

Our story was front-page stuff. It put the focus on Washington-Lee and got it the financial support it needed and deserved.

Wayne Newton

FIRE WORKS

For years—maybe decades—Washington's National Mall was the place to be on the Fourth of July. You know, Times Square on New Year's, the National Mall on July Fourth. It was big fun. Washington's Woodstock. People brought chairs and sofas and staked out their places early. There were kegs and concerts. The Beach Boys were among the headliners. It got a little rowdy, but for the most part it was great fun. I remember doing a live shot on the Mall wearing white pants. While I was on the air, a guy sneaked up and set off a bottle rocket out of my side pants pocket and—boom! swish!—a powder burn down the leg of my trousers. And that wasn't the only stain on my pants.

That particular brand of fun ended in 1983 when Secretary of Interior James Watt decided that the District's Fourth of July celebrations attracted the "wrong element." He decided to change that.

Gone were the sofas.

Gone were the kegs.

Gone were personal fireworks.

Gone were the Beach Boys.

I went into action.

In came Wayne Newton. That's right, good old Danke Schoen himself.

I was there, on the Mall on the Fourth of July, dressed up as my man, Wayne. I was doing a story about how Secretary Watt had stolen our Fourth of July fun and how our national day of celebration would never be the same. Really, when was the last time you rode around in a convertible with the top down blasting "I want some red roses for a blue lady" on the radio?

Sometimes in the world of television, hyperbole works.

Secretary Watt was controversial; his short tenure at the Department of the Interior (1981-1983) was controversial. He had a way with words. He once described his staff as having a black, a woman, two Jews, and a cripple.

What a guy.

GRAPE RESCUES BANANA

Bryan Thompson was 14 years old, a sophomore at Colonial Forge High School. He was not in school that day, he was at his home in Stafford County, Virginia. Why?

School discipline.

Did Bryan steal something at school?

No.

Did Bryan get in a fight at school?

No.

Did Bryan bring a weapon to school?

No.

Bryan had been suspended for ten days for running across the field during halftime at a school football game while wearing a banana outfit. School officials accused him of being disruptive and disrespectful.

The story caught my attention. I interviewed Bryan, I in a Fruit of the Loom grape outfit, and he in his banana outfit. The interview went like this:

Grape: "Why did you decide to do this?"

Banana: "I just wanted to make people happy."

Grape: "Did you realize it would come to this?"

Banana: "No, not at all."

Grape: "Are you sorry?"

Banana: "I guess so—I guess."

Grape: "You won't do it again?"

Banana: "No, I won't be a criminal on the football field."

Grape: "Can I ask you something? Why a banana? Why not a, uh, grape?"

Banana: "I don't know—potassium is great."

At Colonial Forge High School there was a crusade with "Free Banana Man" tee-shirts and coffee mugs. Bryan even composed and performed a free Banana Man rap song.

Grape closed the story, saying: "The school had no comment on this disciplinary action involving a student, but when you think about it, you might see their point. It starts with a banana. Then all of a sudden you have an apple and an orange, or maybe a grape, and before you know it you have fruit salad in the school. And we wouldn't want that."

After the story aired, Bryan's suspension was, well, suspended.

People asked me, "Where did you get that grape outfit?"

"Oh, in my closet, between the strawberry and the orange."

THANK YOU, THANK YOU VERY MUCH

There are roughly 19,000 seats in Washington's Capital One Arena and no matter how the Washington Capitals are doing it's close to a sellout just about every night the Caps play. Hockey fans are loyal, loud, dedicated, and in Washington, long suffering.

It was 2018. The Washington Capitals hockey team was in the Stanley Cup finals, and Washington had championship fever. People who didn't know the difference between the blue line and a blue-light special started paying attention to the Caps.

Elvis and show girls with Stanley's cup (sort of)

The long-suffering Caps made a run for the Stanley Cup. It had made a run for the Cup before. But this time would be different. Year after year the Caps had made the playoffs. Several times they were right on the edge of greatness, only to fall in overtime of the seventh game or go down in some painful, star-crossed way. One famous sportscaster once called them a bunch of "choking dogs." Sometimes the Caps would win the President's Cup, a trophy for the team with the best regular-season record. But winning the President's Cup and not the Stanley Cup is like being named Miss Congeniality rather than winning the crown. The year 2018 would be different: All the team's sins would be forgiven, and all the fans' sorrows would be washed away.

The Caps' opponent in the finals: the Las Vegas Golden Knights. The match was in Las Vegas. I was there – as Elvis (more like fat Elvis). I did the pregame stories with a showgirl on each arm. (C'mon, it's Vegas—we had to do something.) It was big fun. It turns out that Elvis in Vegas is like Santa Claus at Christmas. People would stop gambling in the casino when Elvis walked by. They wanted selfies. Everybody loves Elvis, and I loved being Elvis – for a while. That magic Elvis suit was polyester, and it was 103 degrees. After ten hours it was plastered to me, so much so that I thought I would have to seek medical intervention to have it removed.

Vegas does hockey like Vegas does everything— with glitz and glamour and dancing girls and warring Golden Knights. Vegas won the pregame, but the Capitals skated up when it counted. Washington won the real game—it won the Stanley Cup. DC went wild. That night all the Caps sins were forgiven and the fans' sorrows were washed away. It's good to be Elvis.

COWBOY UP

The city of Washington had long thirsted for some championship champagne. All of a sudden it was drowning in it. First the Washington Capitals won the Stanley Cup in 2018. Then, in 2019, the Washington Mystics won the WNBA Championship, and the underdog Washington Nationals won the World Series, defeating the Houston Astros – in Houston!

I was dispatched to Houston to cover the first two World Series games. It was time to Cowboy Up. I was there with an official Texas cowboy hat, an official Texas cowboy belt, and official Texas red cowboy boots.

Longtime star National's first baseman Ryan Zimmerman got word that I was there and sent word that he wanted to get a picture with me. I didn't have to think twice about that. As it turns out, Zim's wife Heather (his friends call him Zim) grew up in Northern Virginia and was a loyal News 4 watcher. She told her husband that if he ran across Pat Collins to get a picture. So, during batting practice before the world Series game, Ryan Zimmerman and I met. Snap went the shutter. Zim's wife had her photo, and I had a cowboy hat that Zim graciously autographed. What a moment! What a memory.

The Nationals won the first two games in Houston and then suffered three losses at home. Then, the Nats final two wins in Houston brought the World Series trophy home to Washington. It was the first time that Washington was home to the trophy in 95 years.

2019 was a great year for Washington sports – a year Washingtonians will not soon forget.

8

NO INFORMATION, NO STORY

In the television news business there are presenters and then there are reporters. Presenters, their hair always combed and their suits always pressed, are given press releases, go to press conferences, and parrot back the information given to them. Reporters go out and find or try to find new information. It takes persistence. Sometimes it takes a lot of luck. And sometimes you end up empty-handed.

NO DAY AT THE BEACH

To this day I don't know who she was or exactly where she lived. But I do know what she did. You see, earlier that day she had been swimming in the ocean. She went home to shower, and to keep her skin from being damaged by the sun, she rubbed oil all over herself. She was wearing a light sundress, and she was walking towards a Candy Kitchen store, one of those stations of sweetness that sells saltwater taffy, fudge, caramel corn, and other ocean deliciousness. I know all this because I was watching her from a helicopter. I saw it coming, but there was nothing I could really do about it.

But I'm getting ahead of the story.

This story harkens back to the days when Marion Barry was Mayor for Life of Washington DC. Barry had an eye for women. One of those women, an attractive young lady named Grace Shell, was a dancer at a downtown strip club. It was well known that the mayor, accompanied by his entourage of security guards, would show up late at night at Grace's Capitol Hill basement apartment and, well, try to make contact.

These late-night visits didn't sit well with the landlady upstairs, and she blew the whistle, sounded the scandal siren (one of many during those exciting Barry years), and the mayor decided to get out of Dodge.

Oceans Away

Bob Johnson was a good friend of Mayor Barry. He should have been. Barry made him rich. He gave Johnson the Washington DC cable TV contract. Johnson parlayed it into BET, which put him on EASY Street. Bob Johnson had a beach house on the ocean, which was Mayor Barry's hideaway during the Grace Shell scandal.

This all occurred long before we had satellite trucks—long, long, long before LiveU and Dejero devices that allow TV reporters to report from just about anywhere at any time. This was a time when the only way to get from here to there and on the air fast was by helicopter, which put me aloft on that warm day, hovering near that oiled-up woman in the bright sundress.

We arranged to land in the parking lot of the Rusty Rudder, a popular bayside bar. A cab was standing by to take a photographer and me to the beach house. Everything was set.

Well, almost.

Near the Rusty Rudder's parking lot was a volley ball court—a big volley ball court—and the base of that court was beach sand. As the chopper was landing, the backwash of the blades kicked up a sand storm. I yelled to the woman below, "Go inside, go inside!" Of course, she couldn't hear me; she just stood there. By the time we landed, the oiled-up woman in the bright sundress looked like a toasted-almond bar.

I apologized. "I'm sorry," I said, "but I have to go see the Mayor." With that, my photographer and I went off in the cab to track down Mayor Barry on the beach.

The interview went back and forth. I had a lot of questions; Barry had fewer answers. Barry was a masterful politician. He could duck and weave with the best of them and he did, but I got the story.

With sand in my shoes I headed back to the Rusty Rudder. That's when I saw the cops. I thought "Big Trouble," but my apprehension was unfounded. The pilot had gone back to refuel, and the Dewey Beach Police Department had blocked off a stretch of the main highway to accommodate him. Nice. So, into the chopper, up in the air, back to National Airport. We had a live truck waiting. The signal was in. The story went on air. Success!

Sometimes success has a price. As it turns out, there were some cars in that bar parking lot. They were less resilient than the woman in the sundress. Some finishes got finished. The drivers got Maaco. NBC got the bill.

It was worth every penny.

CALEB HUGHES

Part 1: Melissa Brannen Is Missing

Five-year old Melissa Brannen was the cutest little girl. She had a wonderful smile, beautiful hair. She was her mother's pride and joy.

Melissa and her mother lived at the Woodside Apartment complex in Fairfax, Virginia. On December 3, 1989, they went to a Christmas party at the complex's clubhouse. When they were ready to leave around 10 p.m., Melissa ran to get one last scoop of potato chips from the refreshments table. She was never seen again. One minute Melissa was there, and then she wasn't. The police put on a full-court press to find her. They used helicopters; they used dogs. They conducted a door-to-door search over an extensive area.

Early in the case, police started to focus on one suspect. They kept his name close—real close—to the vest.

I got a tip that the person of interest was named Cal. Cal—just Cal. I had three letters and nothing more. CAL. Calvin? I started on Route 1, where the Woodside Apartments were located. I went from business to business, door to door along Route 1, asking if anyone knew or had seen somebody named Cal. Stops at the barbershop, the Merrifield Garden Center, the used car lot, and more yielded nothing.

I stopped at Hillbilly Heaven, an old country-western honky-tonk bar on Route 1. Hillbilly Heaven was owned by Earl Dixon, the father of Donna Dixon, a hot model/actress married to Saturday Night Live star Dan Aykroyd. I went into the bar and asked the question I had been asking all day: "Does anybody here know a guy named Cal?"

EUREKA The bartender knew Cal; Cal had bounced a number of checks at the bar. The bar had kept the checks, and the checks had Cal's name on them.

It turns out Cal was Caleb, not Calvin – Caleb Hughes, the groundskeeper at the Woodside Apartment complex. He was at the Christmas party the night Melissa disappeared. He was police suspect number-one.

Now that I had Hughes' name, I wanted his picture for my story. I needed his address. The bartender remembered that Hughes once worked at a motel down the street, so I decided to give it try. The motel owner not only remembered Hughes, he remembered he had some problems with him. More importantly, the motel owner knew where Hughes lived and he gave me the address.

SUCCESS SQUARED

I wasn't feeling well, having been out the night before to celebrate Tom Sherwood's first anniversary at News 4 and having had a bit more tequila than food. (I helped recruit Sherwood, a Marion Barry expert from the Washington Post. In fact, I produced Sherwood's audition reel. So, after a year, we decided to celebrate.) I needed reinforcements and called my colleague, Jack Cloherty, for help. Jack went to the address and found cops there searching the place. Jack went live and scooped the world. Jack was careful not to say exactly where he was. Hoping to duplicate our story, other stations sent people out to Prince William County to drive around looking for our live truck to trying to find that house.

It didn't work.

Now we knew that the suspect's name was Caleb Hughes and we knew his address, but we didn't know what he looked like. He had not been arrested and charged; he was only a person of interest. We staked out his home with a camera; he didn't leave home.

Figuring that Hughes would open the door for a delivery, I asked one of my bosses to send him a "Pick Me Up" bouquet. When Hughes opened the door, we would get a picture. I thought I had crafted a perfect plan. My photographer and I were there when the delivery man arrived, and we shadowed him as he walked to the door. He knocked. The door opened. A hand reached for the flowers but it was not Caleb's. It was his wife's The flowers may have lifted his wife's spirits that day, but they ruined mine.

That was Strike 1.

My flower ruse had failed, but I would get another chance.

Part 2: Hughes is at Hillbilly Heaven

It was late at night when I got the call. It was Earl Dixon, the owner of Hillbilly Heaven. "He's here now," Earl said," He's in the back-shooting pool."

That's all I needed to hear. I got a late-night crew, headed down Route 1 to Hillbilly Heaven in a live truck, and parked in the Hillbilly Heaven parking lot. I went in by myself. The place was packed, smoke-filled. The pool tables were in the back. From a distance I saw him. Then I went back outside.

Figuring that Hughes had to come out sometime, we staked out the front door, camera at the ready, and we waited. And waited. And waited. You know the song lyrics, "Minutes seem like hours, hours seem like days." That's how it felt that night. Something had to give.

With Dixon's permission, my cameraman Jim Kizer and I went into the bar and snaked our way through the crowd back to the poolroom. I saw Hughes at one of the tables. He saw me. The light above the lens was on, the camera was rolling. I approached Hughes to ask him about Melissa, and he slapped the camera lens away and knocked the microphone to the floor. There was a scuffle I got bit on my hand. We backed off and went outside to see what, if anything, we'd captured on tape. We had captured seconds—maybe five seconds—of foggy, blurry video. No Emmy here.

We continued to stake out the front door. The bar had to close; Hughes had to emerge eventually. He did in the early hours of the morning, surrounded by a scrum of friends, some baring their bottoms, others launching their middle fingers, and shouting things— well, let's just say it wasn't "Good Night." Indeed, it wasn't a good night. Still no picture of Hughes.

All I had to show for that night was a bite wound on my hand. Off to the doctor for a tetanus shot.

Strike 2.

Part 3: Third Time's A Charm

Hughes had a court date in a case unrelated to the Melissa Brannen case. We organized another stakeout. This time I was with cameraman Mike Whatley. This time I drove. Whatley rode shotgun, camera in hand. Whatley was a Vietnam vet. He was a dog handler during the war, and he was fearless. I had no doubt he would get the shot.

We watched as Hughes came out of his Lake Ridge Home, got into his car, and drove to the Manassas courthouse. Whatley got shots of Hughes in the car, getting out of the car, and going into the courthouse. We had enough video for a documentary.

During their investigation, the police found that Hughes, the groundskeeper at the complex, had sat with Melissa and her mother at the Christmas party, talked with them, and even brought a cupcake to Melissa. Although he lived fewer than ten miles from Woodside Apartments, Hughes didn't arrive home until after midnight but couldn't explain why it took him almost three hours to drive home from the party. He denied seeing Melissa and her mother at the party.

When accused of kidnapping Melissa, he told the police investigator to "Prove it."

In November 1990, Hughes was indicted for Melissa's abduction. The prosecuting attorney was Bob Horan. Hughes' trial began in February, 1991. After deliberating for about nine hours over two days, the jury convicted Hughes of abduction with intent to defile. He was sentenced to 50 years in prison. He was released in 2019. Melissa has never been found.

THE DEAL

'I Got Somethin' You Want'

"I got somethin' you want." That's what he said on the phone, and those words got my attention. It was 1986. Len Bias had just died from a cocaine overdose, and I was deep into the case. It was one of those non -stop stories .It seemed that every time I turned around there was another development.

Before I go on with this, I should refresh your memory of Len Bias. Bias was one of the best basketball players to come out of Washington. He moved up and down the court with such grace that it sometimes seemed like his feet didn't touch the floor. Bias was the biggest star that the University of Maryland had produced in years. He was the number one pick in the NBA draft chosen by the Boston Celtics. He was on top of the world, and, then, disaster.

After celebrating his Celtic selection, Bias returned to Washington to link up with friends. He stopped at a liquor store near the Maryland campus, bought a bottle of cognac, and, as it turned out, gave his last autograph to a clerk at the store. Then it was back to Washington Hall on the University of Maryland campus to party with friends and teammates.

It was in that dormitory that Len Bias passed out. A frantic Brian Tribble called 9-1-1. Bias was rushed to Leyland Memorial Hospital, where he was pronounced dead. Brian was not on the team, but he "hung" with the team. He was one of Bias' friends.

There was cocaine at that party—high-quality cocaine. The police seized a bag of coke the size of a fist from a nearby car. Len Bias, the great basketball player on the edge of an incredible professional career, was dead. Dead of a cocaine overdose.

The 'I got somethin' you want' caller said he had the tape of the 9-1-1 call for help made the night Bias died. He wanted to sell it – for cash.

According to station rules—and we have a lot of rules—we cannot pay for interviews. Money can influence what people say, what they do, even how they look. Money can poison a story. But we can, and often do, buy video- and audio- tapes of news events. It's product. It stands on it's own. So when I heard he had the 9-1-1 tape, I was interested—real interested. We arranged to meet.

I felt like I was doing a drug deal. I sat in my car, cash in hand, waiting to score this tape. The bills were crisp. I had been to an ATM, made a withdrawal. I was ready.

The 'I got somethin' you want' caller showed up – with a cassette. I popped it into the tape player and listened. It was about two minutes and ten seconds long, and it was riveting. It sounded legit. Out came the money, off went the man, and back to the station went I with this valuable piece of evidence.

I can't speak for other reporters, but I am paranoid about losing things or not being prepared to work a story. People make fun of me because I carry three or four Sharpies in my pocket, but I will never be at loss for a pen. So, with a high level of paranoia, I delivered the cassette to an editor and asked him to copy it, just in case.

I told you that, to my ear, the tape sounded legit, but just because something sounds legit doesn't mean it's the Real Thing.

A Second Meeting

I knew a lot of people involved in the Bias case. I needed someone I could really trust – someone who had heard the 9-1-1 tape. I needed to speak with someone who wouldn't ask any questions about how I got it.

That led to another meeting with a cop familiar with the case. This time the meet was in a shopping center parking lot. This time in broad daylight. This time the man with knowledge sat in my car. I slipped the tape into the player and then watched as his head nodded while the tape played start-to-finish. I couldn't get back to the station fast enough.

It was probably one of the shortest stories I have ever written. I was live in front of Cole Fieldhouse and simply played the 9-1-1 call made the night Len Bias died.

It was one of those moments when I felt like the whole world was watching.

THE BARRY STING

Just about everybody knew we had it; it drove the other stations crazy. "It" was the now-infamous FBI tape of then-Mayor Marion Barry smoking crack cocaine in a wired room at the Vista Hotel. It was a setup.

Marion Barry had a drug problem. It was well known that he regularly used crack cocaine, a fact that drove a lot of people in law enforcement nuts. They knew he was doing it, but they couldn't prove it. Barry had a security detail, and he used his plainclothes cops as a shield for his down-low meetings to score drugs and sex.

It was also well known that Marion Barry had an eye for the ladies. One of his girlfriends was an attractive African American woman named Rasheeda Moore. Acting as an FBI informant, on January 18, 1990, Moore telephoned Barry and invited him to her room in the Vista Hotel, where the FBI had wired a room with secret cameras and microphones. I think that night Mayor Barry would have gone to the moon to hook up with Rasheeda. Going to the Vista? No sweat.

Rasheeda was waiting in the room with some crack and a pipe. After some casual conversation, Barry asked Moore about drugs. Moore went to the bathroom and returned with a small amount of crack cocaine. Barry told Moore that she should try it first but she replied that it would make her too "hyper." Barry then took two long drags on the pipe, put it down, and reached for his coat. He was using his radio to call his security detail, which was waiting downstairs, when the FBI agents and police swarmed into the room. Down went Barry, uttering the now famous words: "THE BITCH SET ME UP...."

The entire Barry Sting was caught on tape, and I got a copy of that tape – I can't tell you how, though. Other stations complained and shouted: "Make him give it back—make him turn it in!" It got, well, uncomfortable.

The Mayor was to appear in the United States Court for the District of Columbia. TV crews surrounded the Courthouse, photographing all the comings and goings, the prosecutors, the defense attorneys, the witnesses, and, of course, Marion Barry himself. It was intense.

In the midst of all of this, we came up with a sting of our own. My news director, Kris Ostrowski, came to the Courthouse by courier carrying a VHS tape tucked in a folded newspaper. It was not the "Barry Sting Tape," but the rest of the press corps didn't know that. Without saying a word to anyone, we carried the newspaper and that tape into the courthouse.

It was High Noon. One of the stations then 'on air' filmed our tape walk into the Courthouse, and reported that what it had just shown its viewers was proof that we had the "Barry tape" and were finally returning it to the Court,. The reporters on air then rambled on about the tape and Barry. As it continued its "breaking news" broadcast, a man came out of the court and raised his arms in a victory pose. One of the reporters misidentified him as Barry's lawyer celebrating the return of the "tape." It was quite a spectacle. What a sting, except that this time it was not staged by the FBI.

The tape that we had walked into the Courthouse was not the Barry tape but, rather, was a profile of the judge in the case that we had filmed earlier in his chambers. The man with his arms raised in a victory pose was not Barry's attorney but just a guy doing a happy dance. After this embarrassing spectacle, the "Give it back" chants from the other stations went silent. We had the tape, and we aired it before anyone else—with subtitles.

Barry was charged with three felony counts of perjury, ten counts of drug possession, and one misdemeanor count of conspiracy to possess cocaine – even though the cocaine belonged to a government informant. Barry continued as mayor throughout his trial. He was convicted on one drug possession charge arising from a November,1989 incident, but the jury was deadlocked on the remaining charges. Admonishing the jury for not following the instructions that he had delivered prior to their deliberations, Presiding Judge Thomas Penfield Jackson declared a mistrial on these charges. Barry was sentenced to six months in federal prison. He did a victory lap around the Courthouse.

In 1994, Barry once again ran for Mayor of the District of Columbia. He won and was sworn into office on January 2, 1995.

In the following years, Barry had numerous encounters with the law. Prosecutors made a number of runs at Marion Barry, but somehow he always found a way out.

Hadden Clark, big Caps fan, called himself the Rockville Rocket. He would roller skate around handing out advertising fliers for local businesses

CHARLIE AND THE ROCKVILLE ROCKET

Part 1: Laura Houghteling

Charlie Bragale has a knack for listening to police scanners. By the tone of the cop's voice, by a commander's bark, by a dispatcher's urgent directions, Bragale can tell when something big is happening. It was, then, no surprise that Bragale and his cameraman, Luis Urbina, went nearly airborne in a live truck when Bragale heard a call about an arrest on East West Highway. At the scene they found a man standing outside an old pickup truck shouting, for all the world to hear, "I am the Rockville Rocket! I am the Rockville Rocket! I'm the fastest . . . ."

This was the start of what became a twisted murder tale that will not soon be forgotten. Bragale had so many scoops in this ongoing story, it was like a super sundae of news – all about a man named Hadden Clark aka The Rockville Rocket.

Hadden Clark sat at a table in an interview room, tearfully hugging a teddy bear. "We're not going to get away with it this time," he cried. Hadden Clark was about to confess to murder. The cops listened.

His victim was Laura Houghteling, a tall, blonde, 23year-old Harvard graduate who had been stabbed to death in the bedroom of her Bethesda home on October 18, 1992. Clark had worked part-time as a gardener and handyman for Laura's mother, Penny, a psychotherapist. It's believed that Hadden had a thing for Penny and enjoyed the attention she gave him while Laura was away at school. When Laura returned to live at home, Hadden had to compete with Laura for Penny's attention. He was jealous.

When Penny went off to a conference, Hadden Clark went to work on Laura with a kitchen knife, stabbing her multiple times before suffocating her with a pillow. Using a sheet from Laura's bed, Clark removed the body from the house at night and buried it in a shallow grave not far from Laura's home. To make it appear that Laura was still alive, the next morning Clark dressed like a woman, donned a blond wig, and left the Houghteling house. From afar, people might have thought that it was Laura heading off to her job. That ploy worked until police were notified that

Laura had not shown up for work. The cops started searching.

Laura's bedroom was clean. There was no sign of any wrongdoing. Then the police discovered that a bottom sheet and mattress cover were missing from Laura's bed. Using Luminol—a chemical that, under a blue light, can expose traces of blood even after a cleanup—detectives discovered a large blot of blood on Laura's mattress.

The police extended their search. They found a hairbrush containing not only strands of Laura's hair but also strands of artificial hair from a blond wig. Penny Houghteling reported that some of her clothing and jewelry were missing. Most importantly, they found a bloody pillow and pillowcase in the nearby woods. There was a fingerprint on the pillowcase. It was Hadden Clark's.

In November,1992, the police charged Hadden Clark with second degree murder. The police had a murder but no body. Clark refused to tell the police where he had buried Laura. He played games with them, suggesting that he had buried Laura in a State where he had lived as a child,.

In doing so he did not refer to burying "her," he referred to burying "them." With that, the police once again began to look at Clark as a suspect in another case: the abduction of Michelle Dorr, a six-year old girl who disappeared from her father's home on May 31, 1986. Police searched an area in central New Jersey for Laura's and Michelle's bodies but found nothing.

Even prior to his arrest for Laura's murder, Hadden Clark was well known to the police. He called himself the Rockville Rocket. He would strap on roller blades and distribute business fliers around Northwest Washington and nearby Bethesda. He had a criminal record for multiple robberies.

Clark liked to wear women's clothes. He was arrested once for going into a church dressed as a woman and stealing ladies' purses. At his interrogation for the theft, he told the police that he felt like a woman.

Clark attended the Culinary Institute and had a number of cooking jobs, including at the Chevy Chase Country Club, then later as a roller at a bagel shop.

Clark was homeless. Some times he lived out of his pick-up truck and sometimes at a camp site near the spot where eventually they discovered Laura's body.

Clark was one of four children. He spoke his first words when he was five years old: "Me Hadden." Hadden's parents were abusive alcoholics. When Clark was a young boy he was caught breaking into a neighbor's house and putting on her nightie. When kids in the neighborhood angered him, he killed their pets. He was trained as a chef in the Navy but was discharged after being diagnosed a paranoid schizophrenic. While a student at the Culinary Institute when he got angry at a teacher he threatened to pee in the mashed potatoes.

Clark continued to withhold the location of Laura's grave from detectives. He continued to play games with them, hinting that he had killed others and that there was evidence of that near his grandfather's grave on Cape Cod. Montgomery County police organized a search party and headed north. It was January 1993.

Enter again Charlie Bragale, who had been told about the operation. Armed with a number of portable scanners, Charlie, cameraman Jay Alvey, and I climbed in a car and set a land-speed record north. We got to the Cape and spent several days there. We got pictures of the strange search. No bodies discovered, but at one site they found Laura Houghteling's high school ring.

In June,1993, Clark pleaded guilty to Laura Houghteling's murder and sentenced to 30 years in prison. As part of his plea agreement, he told police the location of Laura's body, but the police did not disclose the location to the press or the public. The cops cordoned off a large area. We were there. Bragale had heard some unusual conversation on the scanner and made some well-placed calls, which led us to the woods of an abandoned estate in Bethesda, where the police found Laura's body in a shallow grave.

MISSING

LAURA HOUGHTELING

LAST SEEN SUNDAY, OCTOBER 18, 1992
PLEASE CALL THE MONTGOMERY
COUNTY POLICE AT (301)657-0112
WITH ANY INFORMATION LEADING TO
HER WHEREABOUTS
6 FEET TALL, 145 POUNDS, BROWN
EYES, BLONDE HAIR

Laura Houghteling: first reported missing, later found dead

Part 2: Michelle Dorr

By November, 1992, the police had begun to consider Clark a suspect in the abduction of six year old Michelle Dorr's. Michelle disappeared May 31, 1986.

When Michelle went missing, Michelle's parents, Carl and Deedee, were in the midst of a contentious divorce. On Saturday, May 31, 1986, Michelle was at her father's house in Silver Spring, Maryland. Geoff Hadden and his family lived next door. Michelle and Geoff's daughter, Elizabeth, were friends.

Hadden Clark lived in the basement of Geoff's home until Geoff discovered that Hadden had the disturbing habit of masturbating in the upstairs hallway; he kicked his brother out. On May 31, Geoff took his family out for the day and told Hadden to be gone by the time they returned home. Hadden Clark began packing his belongings in duffle bags.

It was a blistering hot day, and Michelle asked her dad if she could play in the small plastic pool in the backyard. Michelle went outside in her pink, ruffled bathing suit and Carl went back inside. When he checked on Michelle a short time later, she was nowhere to be found.

Michelle's dad called the cops, and they began a search. They circulated fliers. They used search dogs.

When Deedee told the police"Carl did it," Carl became the prime suspect in the disappearance of his own daughter. They questioned him repeatedly. He submitted to two polygraph tests and consented to being hypnotized and to being injected with Amytal Sodium (so-called truth serum). Finally, under extreme pressure, Carl Dorr confessed. Then he recanted. He had a nervous breakdown. The cops watched Carl but never charged him.

When Michelle first disappeared, the police considered Hadden as a possible suspect, but they wrote him off after Carl Dorr's on-again, off-again confessions. Weeks, months, years went by—no sign of Michelle Dorr.

By the time Clark was charged with Laura's Houghteling's murder in 1992, he had become the police's prime suspect in the very troubling Michelle Dorr cold case. At first Clark refused to talk about Michelle Dorr, but his body shook each time the cops mentioned her name.

While in prison for the murder of Laura Houghteling, Clark told another inmate that he had killed Michelle. That was the evidence the cops needed, but it was not enough for a conviction.

In 1995, the police searched a Rhode Island storage locker for evidence relating to Michelle Dorr but found nothing. They once again checked the floorboards in a second story bedroom of Geoff Clark's house. Years had passed since they first checked the house for signs of blood. The house had changed hands a number of times. Although the floor in that upstairs bedroom had been refinished, the police found telltale signs of blood. They submitted the floorboards to a lab for mitochondrial DNA testing. Thanks to Bragale we had a camera crew on the scene to record all the action. It was a decade-old deconstructed crime scene.

On September 23, 1998, the State arrested and charged Clark with Michelle Dorr's murder. After his arrest, he told the cops that Michelle Dorr had come to Geoff's house looking for her friend Elizabeth, that he led the little girl up to a second-floor bedroom and stabbed her, nearly decapitating her. He then took her body to the basement to drain her blood, cut off a piece of her vagina and ate it. He said he cleaned up the murder scene, put the little girl's body in a duffel bag, put the duffel bag in the back of his truck, and went to his cooking job at the Chevy Chase Country Club. He said he later buried Michelle in a wooded area along Route 29.

Hadden Clark was convicted and is serving a 30-year sentence for Michelle Dorr's murder. Until 2000, though, Michelle's body was missing.

On January 8, 2000, Clark led the police to Michelle's grave in a stand of trees about ten miles from her home. Detective Ed Tarney was there. When Tarney looked down and saw a bedspring sticking out of the ground, he asked Hadden, "Is that the spot?" Clark fell to the ground, began clawing at the dirt under the rusted bedspring, and uncovered the skeletal remains of Michelle Dorr in her pink swimsuit. Detective Tarney and his team had worked Michelle Dorr's very cold case for six years. A number of prosecutors and officials had discouraged him from focusing on Clark. "Leave Clark alone," some said. "He had nothing to do with it." Tarney and his team disregarded them all.

High above that crime scene the whirr of a TV helicopter.It was dispatched by Charlie Bragale. He had heard about the discovery on the scanner and dispatched the chopper to get pictures. Finally, the case of the Rockville Rocket was closed.

In jail, Hadden Clark found God. There's actually a video of Clark singing "God's Not Through With Me Yet." Bragale had me write a letter to Clark to see if he would do an interview. Clark wrote back and gave me the name of another inmate to talk to—an inmate who might be more interesting. I think Clark thought I was just looking for a pen pal.

I know this is a tough read, but there is one more important fact that you should know. In 1985, in California,.Clark's older brother Bradfield pleaded guilty to one count of second degree murder and one count of mutilation of human remains. He was charged with the murdering a woman, cutting her up, and eating one of her breasts, which he had barbecued on a charcoal grill. The rest of her was found in the trunk of his car.

9

THE UNSOLVED

Many of the murders I have written about were high-profile cases, front-page stories that gained a lot of attention. But, regrettably, many murders in our area are not solved and don't get front page attention. They *might* get a two or three paragraph story in the back of the paper or a short mention in a newscast. But these little reported murders are just as vicious, their victims are just as dead, and the victims' relatives are just as hurt as in the case with high profile murders that get the full Law and Order treatment. These are some of the murders I remember that remain unsolved at this writing.

DANA CHISHOLM, FEBRUARY 17, 1995

Not to make this sound like a corny murder-mystery novel, but it was a cold, rainy February day in 1995 when I was wandering about the murder scene of Dana Chisholm in Northwest Washington DC. I was following one of my reporting rules: Always visit the murder scene. Murder scenes have a macabre magnetism about them. There you will find the victim's relatives and friends, interested parties, and sometimes even suspects. Never ignore the scene. On that cold, rainy morning I found a key on the street – a key to Dana Chisholm's basement apartment. It was a key to the murder scene. The killer had dropped it.

Murder was a stranger in this safe, upscale Crestwood neighborhood. Nearby was the sprawling Rockefeller estate; a few doors down, the home of retired FBI director William Sessions.

Dana Chisholm, 25, a secretary at a Washington think tank, was from Rock Hill, South Carolina. Dana had come to Washington to launch her career and be part of the scene in the Nation's Capital. She rented a basement apartment in a large home on Argyle Terrace—an apartment with a separate entrance. On the evening of February 17, 1995, someone entered through the basement door and killed Dana.

Dana's landlady found her body about 20 hours after her death. She had been strangled. According to those familiar with the scene, Dana was found naked with a cord around her neck, the cord tied to a doorknob. She had been bathed and made up.

The killer left a note at the scene: "MPD best pussy in town. I'll be back."

In and around the city of Washington DC, only people in or closely associated with law enforcement refer to the DC police department as the MPD. The fact that MPD was used in that note indicated the killer had some familiarity with the Metropolitan Police Department.

Dana's Rolodex was missing—a good sign that the killer's name and number were in it. Also missing from the scene was Dana's key to her apartment.

Dana was described as a loyal and talented worker. At night she had an active social life, a very active social life. She was a regular at clubs and dated guys she met through advertisements in the City Paper. She got caught up in the fast-paced nightlife, the world of Washington so much different than her hometown of Rock Hill. I met one of Dana's nighttime friends, a woman with a flower tattoo in her ear, at a bar near DuPont Circle. She told me about Dana's activities— some of Dana's activities but not everything. The meeting went on for some time. She promised to get back to me, but then she disappeared. In a way, Dana's nightlife was like a Rubik's Cube, little blocks of this and that—people familiar with one or two blocks, but no one could twist the whole story together.

Dana was devoted to her father. She called him just about every day. Apparently, the killer knew that. Within hours after the murder, the killer called Dana's dad in South Carolina and identified himself as a DC detective. He told Dana's dad that he had arrested her for prostitution, but that she was all right. He said she would be held in jail for a couple of days and that he shouldn't worry if she didn't call for some time.

From a pay phone near the police station the killer made another call, this time to a homicide detective working the case. He told the cop he would tell him all about the murder if—if—IF the cop held a news conference to announce that Dana Chisholm was a prostitute. He gave the detective a code name so he would know the caller if they were to talk again. He said, "Call me Spiderman." The police put ads in the City Paper trying to lure Spiderman into the open, but, in spite of several attempts, nothing. Investigators checked up and down the East Coast to see if there were similar murders with similar victims. Nothing. They ran through possible known sex offenders to see if they could find any connection. Nothing.

VIVIAN MARROW, JANUARY 18, 2017.

In broad-daylight, the 68-year-old mother of three and grandmother of 11, was gunned down in her wheelchair as she was on her way to the corner store. It happened on Elvans Road in Southeast DC. Violence is no stranger there. Police believe there was some sort of gunfight and Vivian was caught in the crossfire. She was an innocent victim, and the crime scene was haunting: A wheelchair – Vivian's wheelchair – behind crime-scene tape.

GRANT DOSUNMU, DECEMBER 11, 2016.

Grant Dosunmu was DC through-and-through. He attended Lafayette Elementary, Deal Middle School, and Woodrow Wilson High. Grant wanted to be an entrepreneur like his father, but that dream ended in bloodshed on 32nd Street, Northwest. Grant was shot and killed behind the wheel of his Jaguar, a gift from his father, about a block and a half from his home in the Hawthorne section of the city. Grant was 21.

LUKE HOLT, APRIL 6, 2015.

When officials boast about economic development in our City, they're not likely to show pictures of an old apartment-housing development on 37th Street, Southeast about half a block away from the gleaming Washington Nationals Youth Baseball Academy. The building is in a neighborhood in decay where shoes dangle over power lines. Here and in other areas of our City, neighborhood crews tie the laces of shoes together and drape the shoes over the power lines above to mark the spot where something bad happened or is happening. Sometimes it signals a drug market nearby. Sometimes it serves as a marker for murder. So unnerving are these shoes in the sky that the City sends workers out to cut them down. It was on the steps of the old apartment building that Luke Holt was shot and killed. He was 16 years old. Witnesses say a car came down the street, its sunroof opened, and a gunman stood up in the opening and fired six shots. Luke Holt fell dead to the ground. Not far away – shoes in the sky.

PHILLIP JONES, JANUARY 14, 2015.

Phillip Jones, 17, was shot and killed at the intersection of Martin Luther King Jr. Avenue and Randall Place, Southeast. Jones had just left a basketball game at nearby Ballou High School, and minutes later he was dead in the intersection. When he died, Jones was preparing to join the Job Corps. Those plans died with him at that intersection.

ANTHONY LARRY LEAK, DECEMBER 4, 2014.

People who knew Anthony say his infectious smile could bring joy to a room. The Lincoln University graduate had a lot going for him. He sold insurance. He mentored kids with special needs. His father said there was no downside to his life. Anthony Leak was shot to death inside his Cadillac. The crime scene: Anacostia Avenue in Northeast DC. You see, to make extra money Anthony Leak worked as a courtesy car driver, picking up people at a nearby Safeway store and taking them and their groceries to their homes. It's a transportation system that's been in play in the City for years. Anthony had been doing it since he was a teenager. That courtesy job likely cost him his life.

JAMES OH, JULY 4, 2014.

Customers and neighbors called him "Pop Pop" and "Mr. James." He ran the Gold Corner Market for years and years. On Independence Day in 2014, two men walked into the store wearing hooded sweatshirts and masks. They pushed Mr. Oh's wife aside, grabbed money from the cash register, and then savagely attacked Mr. Oh. Mr. Oh was taken to a hospital where he died a short time later. James Oh was 76 years old.

MARY HOUSTON, MAY 7, 2014.

Mary Houston was a churchgoing, fashion-conscious mother of four and grandmother of 13. She was found murdered in the basement of a vacant warehouse on Channing Place, Northeast, about two blocks from her home. Mary Houston was 75 years old. At the time of her death, she was suffering from Alzheimer's. Her family says from time to time she would wander off but always came back. This time was different.

ROBERT WONE, AUGUST 2, 2006

This is not a low-profile case; in fact, due to the circumstances surrounding the murder, it was a very high-profile case. A man was killed; three people were present; yet no one has ever been charged with murder.

Racks.

Metal shackles.

Leather collars.

Wrist and ankle restraints.

Mouth gags.

Black spandex hoods.

Assorted clamps and clips.

Black clothespins.

Enema kit.

Penis rings.

Penis vices.

Assorted metal chains with locks.

Studded penis binding.

Dildos.

Butt plugs.

Nipple suction devices.

Electrical shock devices.

Devices to force the wearer to drink another's urine.

Books relating to inflicting pain on others and/or enslaving others for sexual gratification.

These were some of the items seized by police from 1509 Swann Street, Northwest, a million-dollar row house where Robert Wone was murdered.

Wone was a 32-year-old attorney who lived with his wife in Oakton, Virginia. Wone planned to work late on August 2, 2006 and arranged to stay at the Swann Street house with his college friend from William and Mary, Joe Price. He had told his wife that he would spend the night in the city with some friends. Wone arrived at the Swann Street house around 10:30 p.m. It turned out to be the last night of his life.

Neighbors reported hearing a scream around 11:35 p.m. The scream came from housemate Victor Zaborsky's. Then, shortly before midnight, Zaborsky called 9-1-1. He told the operator that an "intruder" had stabbed a guest inside the house at 1509 Swann Street. According to Court documents, Zaborsky volunteered that "the person had one of our knives."

The Threesome

We must begin with the three men who lived 1509 Swann Street. Joe Price was a partner at the Arent Fox law firm. Dylan Ward was a masseur. Victor Zaborsky was an advertising man involved in the "Got milk?" mustache campaign.

Court documents indicate that Price, Zaborsky, and Ward had a polyamorous relationship. Price and Zaborsky shared the master bedroom in a committed and intimate pairing. Ward had a bedroom of his own but had an intimate personal relationship with Price. Theirs was a dominant/submissive sexual relationship,

Ward being the dominant partner and Price the submissive one. Investigators confirmed this with photos from Price's computer.

Prosecutors said that all three men were very close and had a motive to protect each other's interests. In an interview with the cops, Zaborsky said Ward could not have killed Wone because Ward was one of the "nicest, sweetest people I have ever met."

In Court documents and in private interviews, officials said that Robert Wone was heterosexual, happily married, and had no sexual or intimate relationship with any of the three men who lived in the Swann Street house. All three Swann Street men went to Robert Wone's funeral; Joe Price was a pallbearer.

The Death Scene

Robert Wone was found lying on his back, his hands at his sides, his head on a pillow on a pullout couch in the second-floor guestroom of the Swann Street house. He was wearing a gray William and Mary T-shirt, gym shorts, and underwear. His other clothes were neatly folded on a nearby table. Wone's wallet, Movado watch, and Blackberry were in plain sight. On a bedside table lay a bloody knife that appeared to have been removed from a knife set in the kitchen.

Medics who responded to the murder scene described the behavior of the three men in the house as "odd." One medic said it made the hair on the back of his neck stand up. They found three stab wounds in Wone's chest but little or no blood near the stab wounds. There was no sign of any disturbance in the room. The bed had been made, the sheet and comforter turned down at a 45-degree angle. One medic noted that it appeared that Wone had been stabbed, showered, redressed, and put in bed.

In Dylan Ward's room investigators found a New Yorker magazine opened to an article entitled "Late Works," a story about how people used to die in their homes. Illustrating the article was a full-page drawing of Shakespeare lying dead in bed, his body position similar to Robert Wone's.

Investigators believed that the lack of blood at the scene, the lack of signs of a struggle by Wone, and the marks on his neck were suspicious. They believed that the defendants had tampered with the crime scene and that the actual murder weapon was possibly a knife missing from a set in Ward's room rather than the kitchen knife found near the murder scene.

The Medical Examiner – the ME – described the stab wounds as clean, symmetrical, uniform—the wounds appeared to have been "methodically inflicted. The ME found several needle marks on Wone's body and puncture marks on his neck, his chest, and his foot. According to the ME, the needle marks were made before Wone died. The ME determined that the medical evidence firmly established that Wone was alive and incapacitated at the time the stab wounds were inflicted, which explains why there were no defensive wounds on his body.

The visual painted by the ME was haunting: Robert Wone was somehow paralyzed, stabbed three times in the chest, and remained alive for a considerable period of time. His fluids spilled into his stomach, and he began digesting his own blood. The ME found no traces of paralyzing drugs in Wone's body, though it's been said the ME didn't test for some of the drugs that could have done the job. The ME did, however, find semen on Wone's ass, inside his rectal canal, on his thighs and genitals. The DNA of the semen was tested and found to be Wone's own. The doctor believes this was evidence that Wone was sexually assaulted.

The Threesome And Their Story

When the police arrived at the Swann Street house they found Price, Zaborsky, and Ward in the living room wearing what they described as crisp white robes, "appearing as if they'd just showered." The three were taken in for questioning.

All three men repeated the same story about what happened that night. In this serious game of Clue the threesome said," The burglar did it." They all said a burglar scaled the security fence in the back, entered the house through an unlocked back door, took a knife from the kitchen, climbed the stairs to the second-floor guestroom, stabbed Robert Wone to death, and left the house the way he came in.

You might wonder why a burglar would enter the house, murder Wone, and then leave, stealing nothing—not Wone's wallet, his expensive watch, or the pricey electronics in the living room. A burglar who took a knife from the kitchen, murdered a man on the second floor of a house when three men were in the house and then left with nothing?

Criminal Charges

In the first year after the murder, the case was transferred to three different federal prosecutors. The widow was frustrated with what she considered to be police inaction. The Organization of Chinese Americans was frustrated. The Attorney General of the United States pleaded publicly with Price, Ward, and Zaborsky to cooperate with the police.

It was not until October,2008, two years after Wone's murder, that the federal prosecutor filed an affidavit, probably one of the most well-read affidavits in Washington crime history, to support Dylan Ward's arrest on an obstruction of justice charge. At that time, Dylan was living in Florida in a house owned by Price. In November, Price and Zaborsky were charged with obstruction, and on December 19, 2008, the prosecutor filed conspiracy charges against all three men. The defendants were represented by high-profile, well-known defense attorneys.

The Trial

Believing that testimony about their S&M sex activity and the prosecutor's introduction of the items listed above into evidence at a trial could bias the jurors. With that in mind the defense lawyer opted for a bench trial rather than put the case in the hands of a jury. This proved to be a good decision.

Lynn Lebovitz was the judge. She graduated with a B.A. in religious studies from Brown University and a J.D. from Georgetown University. A former prosecutor, she was appointed by President George W. Bush in

2001 as an associate judge on the Superior Court of the District of Columbia.

The trial began May 17, 2010. It lasted about a month. I was at the trial every day; a lot of reporters were at the trial every day. The trial was so intriguing that a group of citizen journalists did a live blog of it every day.

The government argues that the defendants altered and orchestrated the crime scene, planted evidence, delayed reporting the murder to the police, and lied to the police about the true circumstances of the murder. The prosecutors introduced thirty witnesses and hundreds of exhibits, including a mockup of the Swann Street house.

Each day the Swann Street threesome showed up in their Sunday best. I would look at them, think about all the sex toys the cops seized, and wonder what the hell was going on in that Swann Street house. Sometimes there was a feeling of tension in the courtroom as we waited for a Perry Mason moment, but that moment never came.

Lawyers for the defense began their case on June 17. None of the Swann street threesome took the stand.

On June 29, Judge Leibovitz found each defendant not guilty of the charges of conspiracy, obstruction of justice, and tampering with evidence. In explaining her ruling from the bench, she said she believed the defendants knew who killed Robert Wone but that she was not convinced beyond a reasonable doubt that they committed the offenses with which they were charged.

Being found not guilty beyond a reasonable doubt is not the same as being found totally innocent beyond a reasonable doubt. Is it?

So who killed Robert Wone? I will tell you who didn't. The killer wasn't a burglar who climbed over the security fence, went through the open back door of the Swann Stret house, grabbed a knife from the kitchen, went upstairs to the guest bedroom, committed a bloodless stabbing, and then left the Swann Street house empty-handed.

Civil Action

On November 25, 2008, Kathie Wone filed a $20-million wrongful-death suit against Ward, Price, and Zaborwky. In August, 2011, five years after Robert Wone was killed in the Swann Street house, the parties settled out of court on for an undisclosed sum.

10

THE SNOW STICK AND OTHER STORIES

BEING CATHOLIC

I remember what it was like to be Catholic.

I remember the nine First Fridays, followed by hot chocolate and honey-dipped donuts—and the promise of everlasting happiness. I remember "*Ad deum qui laetificat juventutem meam*," swigging down some altar wine, and racing other altar boys to finish the Suscipiat. I remember the sore knees, the hardwood floors, the Hail Marys, the Our Fathers. But I still can't recall the joyful mysteries. I have always had trouble with them.

I had a chance to serve one of the first low Masses at the Basilica of the National Shrine of the Immaculate Conception – the National Shrine – shortly after construction was completed. Every pew, every seat was filled. The altar was huge. The bell that I had to ring was enormous. I needed to use both hands just to swing it back and forth.

All seemed to be going well. Then it happened. My cassock caught the bell's handle, and the bell took off, tumbling down the marble stairs. I chased it, but it was out of my reach. It fell and fell, its ding dong ding dong seemed deafening in the silenced church. Finally, it came to rest on the floor well below the altar. With one fist I grabbed the handle. With the other fist I grabbed the clapper. I looked up and saw the priest's face – red as my cassock.

My Shrine altar boy debut had turned into my Shrine altar boy finale.

I remember what it was like to be Catholic. The fasting rules, the rights and wrongs, Heaven and Hell. I remember it seemed like an old-time religion in a modern-day world.

I remember what it was like to be Catholic. Falling away, reckless freedom, no responsibility. People would joke about buying the movie rights to my confession. "Bless me, Father, it's been a long, long time now—at my age physically incapable of breaking at least five of the Ten Commandments."

I remember what it was like to be Catholic. My beloved Notre Dame had a fierce rivalry with the University of Miami – Catholics versus Convicts. Miami's coach Jimmy Johnson brought a priest, and an Irish priest at that, to one pregame banquet. To the assembled crowd the priest said, "God really doesn't care who wins that game tomorrow."

Notre Dame coach Lou Holtz, always quick on his feet, responded, "God may not care—but his Mother does."

I remember what it was like to be Catholic. Every time I see a victim of violence, every time I look into the tear-stained eyes of the relatives left behind. Knowing that each time we tell a story about death, we are really celebrating a life. Precious. Fragile. Sacred.

I remember my revival. My wife keeps track of the exact date. On Saturday October 3, 1992, Stanford beat Notre Dame 33-16. The next Sunday I started going back to Mass. Was it because of my age? Or was it because of that devastating defeat?

Then came the church sex scandals. First in Boston, then in other cities. Then here in Washington DC. Defrocked Cardinal McCarrick became Mr. McCarrick. There were stories about sexual assaults and McCarrick's secret slush fund and payments made to church officials, all the time the church's moral authority slipping away.

I still go Mass.

But I keep reminding myself there is more to the church than the priests.

I am a Catholic. I will always remember that.

Now, Mother Mary, can we please find a way to beat Clemson?

THE STICK

It was February 5, 2010. There she was, like a vision appearing in the whirlwind of snow, at first just a shadowy outline lit by the glare of the streetlight, moving towards me—make that gliding towards me. As she got closer and closer I could see more: a round mink hat; a smart, short winter jacket; skintight, flesh-

The original snow stick

In the snow with the Pat Collins Snow Stick

*In a snowball fight with Mayor Marion Barry. His snow
removal plan could be described in one word... Spring*

*more snow,
more stick...*

colored leggings. Her name was Brenda. She was all alone. It was early. It was snowing hard, and she was about to become the talk of the town. We spoke.

Me: "So what brings you out here in all this snow?"

Brenda: "I came out to get some coffee."

Me: "There's not much open—just the Exxon station down the street."

Brenda: "That's where I will go."

Me: "Sure, 'cause when I think about coffee, I always think of Exxon."

There was something alluring about Brenda – perhaps everything: Her uptown attitude. Her upscale outfit. The mink hat that she confided had come from an ex-husband. Brenda was a little Marilyn Monroe, a little Mae West. And the graceful way she moved about—well, she almost used the snow as a prop.

Brenda was the opening act in what turned out to be something known as Snowmageddon. More than 12 hours of wall-to-wall TV coverage of a snowstorm in Washington, DC.

Snow is a big deal in Washington, DC. It's a city stopper. You'd think nuclear waste was falling from the sky. All of a sudden people forget how to drive. They race to the grocery store for milk, toilet paper, paper towels, and eggs. Schools close. The governments close. In Washington DC, the most powerful city in the world, snow is kryptonite. People from Buffalo mock us. People from Chicago ridicule us. In every place with "serious snow" we are a laughingstock.

When Marion Barry was mayor, the snow plan for Washington could be described in one word: Spring. He would say the good Lord brought the snow, the good Lord will take it away. We have always had a troubled relationship with snow. So when there is even a hint of the white stuff in the forecast, it's an all-hands-on-deck alert at TV stations. Hotel rooms are booked. Days off are canceled. Hand warmers are passed around. We suffer so you don't have to.

So, on that February morning, I was at John Conner's gas station at the intersection of Connecticut Avenue and Fessenden Street, Northwest, my snow stick in hand, and Brenda at my side.

I was at Conner's because that's where our live truck was taken to have a broken water pump repaired. We couldn't drive the truck, but we could go live from it, and that's what we needed to do every 15 minutes, every hour— I, became your human weather station, measuring snow and talking to people as they passed by. The snow fell quickly. There were three inches and then five inches. I can hear the people from Chicago laughing already.

In these whiteout conditions another figure appeared—this time a woman in blue. Now the snow was really coming down. It wasn't Buffalo bad, but if you stood on one corner it was hard to make out the WALK/DON'T WALK sign on the other. Low visibility really didn't matter because there was only an occasional car creeping slowly by. The Lady in Blue and I spoke.

Me: "So what brings you out in this stuff?"
Lady in Blue: "I have to go to the Giant."
Me: "Which Giant?"
Lady in Blue: "The one in Friendship Heights."
Me: "That's about two miles away."

Lady in Blue: "I know—but I have a coupon for a free sandwich."

Me: "You are going to walk two miles in the snow for a sandwich?"

Lady in Blue: "Yes, I have a coupon."

With that and a great sense of purpose, the Lady in Blue left me. She headed down the street and disappeared behind a curtain of white flakes, sandwich on her mind, coupon in her pocket, gloves on her hands.

In many ways snow can bring a great sense of peace to a city. It can force you to step away from the rigors of work, walk away from the computer, put down the iPhone, look out the window, and get to know people you should have known all along, like neighbors and even your own family members.

At the corner of Fessenden and Connecticut, my snow count continued: seven inches; nine inches. Cabin fever began to set in—and people emerged. Kids came by. One claimed to have brought the snow by sleeping in his pajamas inside out. A little girl said the snow shark created Snowmageddon. My measuring spot became something of a destination for people who had been watching our comings and goings on TV all day long. So many dogs came by that we could have done a entire segment on "Best in Snow." Then came the generous people with food: matzo ball soup; subs; hot chocolate; pizza; burgers; fries—a buffet of deliciousness spread out along the snowy sidewalk. Traditionally we measure snow in inches. This storm I measured in pounds as well.

Connecticut Avenue, usually a thoroughfare of bumper-to-bumper traffic, had become a snowy boardwalk for brave, bundled-up, winter-storm warriors. Off in the distance I saw the Lady in Blue, trudging down the Avenue. She approached, bag in hand. She had made it to that Giant Food store, cashed in her coupon for the free sandwich, and was on her way home with her sandwich when she had become slightly disoriented and lost in the heavy snow. But she had soldiered through it and was now only steps away from her home. She unwrapped her trophy sandwich on live television for all the world to see. The cheese had curled, the meat had drooped, the bread was limp. It looked more like a biology experiment than lunch. But she got it and made it home with her ten fingers and ten toes intact, her mission accomplished.

The snow continued to fall at the intersection of Connecticut Avenue and Fessenden Street, and we continued to count: 11 inches, 12 inches—on and on.

Why measure the snow?

Americans are all about keeping score: bigger, better, stronger, taller, heavier numbers are all about how we define our lives. Measuring snow is a way to measure our storms. For some it's a measurement of magic, for others a misery index, but a measurement, nonetheless. And though most official snow totals are recorded at nearby airports, over the years we've noticed that airport totals often differ substantially from what we see on the streets where we live. So we prefer our live, homegrown measurements to those airport numbers. After all, it's not rocket science. Is it?

So, what's with the stick?

The original snow stick—a four-sided yardstick handed out years ago by the old C&P Telephone Company—was a measuring instrument my daughter Salley was given at school. She brought it home as a keepsake, but as I began to track snowstorms on television, I seized the stick to measure snow all around the City, snow after snow after snow. If you look closely you can see the wear and tear on the tip of the stick. Snowmageddon changed all that.

Over that two-day storm, the TV viewership was through the roof, and Mona Naboli—a creative genius at News4—came up with an idea to craft an official Pat Collins Snow Stick. It was big and blue and, in addition to the traditional 36-inch measurements, it had markings noting the big snows from our city's past. It was the official Pat Collins Snow Stick—the only real, true way to measure snow in the city of Washington. There was a little bit of history, a little bit of reality, all right there in the Pat Collins Snow Stick.

We didn't stop with my new Snow Stick. With each snow we came up with a special snow-stick challenge: Best snow man. Best snow hat. Best in snow. People from all over would do something creative with the snow or in the snow, photograph it, and enter to win. We'd have a panel of judges, and, using an Olympic scoring system, we would select a winner and then present the winner with his or her very own official Pat Collins Snow Stick.

People like the stick. People want the stick. We've had requests to sell it. We've had requests to donate it for charity auctions. But winning a challenge is the only way to get an official Pat Collins Snow Stick.

So, when we get a stick-worthy snow, I'll be back at Connecticut and Fessenden, measuring snow, and waiting for Brenda.

I'll see you there.

Chuck Bell predicts it... I have to stand in it

CHUCK BELL

From the time he was seven years old, Chuck Bell knew he wanted to be a weatherman. In fact, he can pinpoint the exact day: April 4, 1974, the day ending a 24 hour period with the second largest – but most violent – tornado outbreak in recorded history in North America. During the 1974 Super Outbreak 148 tornados touched down in 13 States and one Canadian province. The one hundred twenty seventh tornado went right over Mount View Elementary School in Albany, Georgia, where Chuck Bell and his classmates crouched in a duck-and-cover position in the school hallway. After that, all Chuck wanted to do was talk about the weather. And Chuck can talk. In fact, when he talked too much, his mother, a grade-school teacher, would tell him to go read an encyclopedia, and Chuck would go off to the bookshelf for some quiet time.

Chuck is smart. He got 740 out of a possible 800 on his college boards. His parents wanted him to go to Auburn, but Auburn didn't have a school of meteorology. Without his parents' knowledge, Chuck applied to the University of Oklahoma. When his parents and he visited the campus, they were rousted from their beds at 2 a.m. by a severe storm with 60-mile-per-hour winds, rain, and hail. Chuck told his parents the storm was "awesome." Chuck received a partial scholarship, and off he went to Norman, Oklahoma. For a while, Chuck had flirted with the idea of becoming an airline pilot but he had always been fascinated by weather, and the study of meteorology won out. Chuck says a meteorologist is just a pilot with bad eyesight. Chuck wears glasses.

Chuck is a numbers man. In high school he was on the math team. When he pledged a fraternity, the frat brothers told Chuck to do something no one else could do. In response he recited flawlessly the license plate number of each of the frat brothers. That's a numbers man.

While in college, Chuck interned at various TV outlets. After his graduation, Chuck began the small-market TV news pilgrimage, doing weather along the way. In Greenville, South Carolina, he was the purveyor of Chuck's Coffee Club Mugs. He did weather in Roanoke and in Oklahoma City. For Sinclair Broadcasting he did weather for three stations: Cincinnati, Raleigh, and Oklahoma City.

Chuck joined NBC4 in Washington in 2009, where he got what is called the "double double," meaning weekend mornings and nights from 3:30 a.m. to 11:30 p.m. That schedule lasted four-and-a-half years—or what Chuck calls "forever."

Chuck Bell is a terrific weatherman, and, as I said before, he is smart. He is witty. He is glib. And he is gay. He was one of the first local TV personalities to come out. That was not an easy decision; Chuck says that earlier in his career he was fired from one job because he was gay and denied another because of it. "I knew I was gay my whole life," Chuck says. "I never had any doubt about who I was attracted to."

On October 11, 1991, Chuck went to visit his mom on her birthday. "I told her I'm gay." She started to cry. Chuck said "I told her 'Don't cry, Mom, I'll be fine.'" He said "My mom told me, 'I'm not sad. Now I have to have a different dream for your life.'" In 2005 Chuck met Eric Klein at a gay nightclub in Northwest DC. Later came a commitment ring. Viewers started asking questions and Chuck started talking openly on the air about his better half. The two married in Paris in 2015.

Now Chuck's day job begins at 1:30 a.m. He says that he drags himself out of bed, gulps down two cups of coffee, and arrives at NBC4 at 2:40 a.m., The first thing he does is check his score: Did yesterday's weather prediction happen today?Chuck needs to know.

Does every weatherman do that? "Not every one," says Chuck, "but I'm a numbers person."

By the way, Chuck's number is 85—meaning he's accurate an impressive 85 percent of the time.

RED-FACED REPORTER

Don't Make Stuff Up

I was short—about five inches short—and it was late at night. Or should I say early in the morning—perhaps two or three a.m. I was 17 and in charge of editing three pages of high school sports for the Washington Daily News. All the stories had been stacked and shipped and, yet, there was a five-inch hole in one of the pages.

I needed something for that hole, so I wrote a story about an imaginary game between two imaginary schools, and—what the hell—I gave myself a byline: Tap Snilloc. That would be Pat Collins backwards. Hole filled. Time to go to press.

I thought it was humorous, but Michael Bernstein, my boss, didn't see it that way. He was all over my ass. His words to me "We don't make up games. We don't make up stories. We don't make up bylines."

I got it. I got it. I got it. Lesson learned.

Nellie Snilloc

Fast-forward about nine years. I had just started in television at Channel 9 in Washington. At the start of my career, I wasn't just bad—I was terrible. Everyday Jim Snyder, the news director, would call me into his office and go over my stories. It was tough, unvarnished, and often led to three-scotch nights. One day during this initiation period, Synder walked – make that marched – no, make that stomped – out of his office straight towards my desk in the newsroom. In his hand was a small white piece of paper upon which were some handwritten words.

They said," So happy you have added Pat Collins to your reporting staff. His stories are so very interesting." Snyder's hand shook as he waved the letter in front of my face. "We do not solicit fan mail," Snyder said. "This is bullshit—you know who sent this?"

First of all, let me tell you that my mother had very distinctive handwriting. It was better than the Palmer method. I would describe it as Palmer-plus. All I had to do was look at the first line to know the author of that flattering little note.

"You know who sent this letter?" Snyder asked again.

"No clue," I said. "No clue."

Snyder balled it up and threw it into the trash and walked away.

Oh, did I mention that it was signed, "Nellie Snilloc?"

Those Snillocs have a way of popping up at the most inopportune times.

Jim is Watching

It was a Saturday and I was still a relatively new TV reporter. When you are new, weekends are the way you pay your dues. And on this particular weekend there was a big Kennedy family affair at Holy Trinity Church in Georgetown. I was there to cover it live, filming and talking about the various dignitaries as they filed into the church. As I ran down the list of the important, I got to Eunice Kennedy Shriver, but as I broadcast her name it came out, "You Neece."

Now I have to tell you, when Jim Snyder was news director, he watched everything. Even on the weekends. They didn't have speed dial back then, but we swore he would sit at home and dial up the first six numbers to the control room, and if he saw something he didn't like, he would hit the seventh number and boom! You'd hear from him.

That Saturday the call came to me. "What was going through your mind?" he said. "How could you possibly call her You NEECE?"

"Well, Jim, I was probably thinking of her sister-in-law EEThel."

MEETING MARILYN

On to Chicago, where I spent three years doing feature stories for WLS-TV. None was quite like the day-in-the-life of Marilyn Chambers.

If there were a porn star hall of fame, Marilyn would be right there at the head of the class. There was a time that porn films—or, as some people like to call them, dirty little movies—were confined to peep-show arcade booths: 25 cents for 15 seconds, in black-and-white with the "stars " wearing masks and socks and little else. Then came color and production and named porn stars.

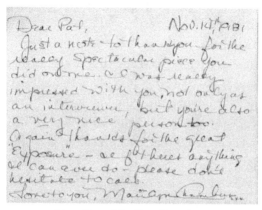

Note from Marilyn Chambers

Marilyn Chambers was a barrier-breaker—attractive, clean-cut, all-American. My god, she was the woman pictured on the box of Ivory Snow. More than that, Marilyn was the star of Behind the Green Door, one of the most famous porn movies of all time. It actually played in theaters where moviegoers didn't use Groucho glasses to disguise themselves.

Marilyn came to Chicago, and I set out to do a day-in-the-life of a porn star. She was staying in a high-floor suite of a well-known hotel. My cameraman and I went to her room, and something like this followed:

Knock on door.

"Who's there?"

"Pat Collins, WLS-TV."

The door opened.

There stood Marilyn—Marilyn Chambers there in the doorway. Marilyn Chambers there in the doorway wearing a sheer robe. And nothing else.

Wow.

"Want to see the ring Sammy Davis Jr. gave me?" she asked.

"Sure," I said.

Then she parted her robe, lifted one of her legs, and there it was—the ring. In a place I didn't expect to see a ring. Marilyn had one. She had her, well—she had it pierced, and there was the ring, like a tiny tree topper. I never really had an interview start like that before.

She was smart – and cordial. Before she left town she sent me a note thanking me for the exposure.

SOUPY

Washington, DC. WJLA-TV. Another sort of day-in-the-life assignment. The subject: Soupy Sales.

Now, depending on how old you are, you might have to ask your parents, or even grand-parents, about Soupy Sales. Know this: He was a very popular comedian. He had his own TV show. He had a couple of off-color jokes that made

> FRI NOV 2
> DEAR PAT –
> JUST A SHORT NOTE
> to thank you For that
> wonderful spot on the
> 11: O'clock news. I
> saw it and loved it!
> You certainly helped
> us sell out this
> weekend.
>   It was also nice
> to meet you and you
> edited the price so
> great. Again my thanks
> Pat. Hope to see you
> again soon . SOUPY SALES

Note from Soupy Sales

him world-famous, like: "I took my girlfriend to a base-ball game. I kissed her on all the strikes and she kissed me on—well, you get the idea.

Soupy Sales was a character and on the back nine of his career, which brought him to a Washington DC comedy club.

Doing a feature on a comic is pretty straight-forward: Interview him backstage during the day, shoot the act at night, and intercut his thoughts about life and his jokes about life and—voila! —,a nice, thoughtful story.

The day of Soupy's performace I interviewed him. That night I went to the club to shoot his act. Even though Soupy was up in years and his bit somewhat old, he was a headliner and the last act on the bill.

I got there early and sat at the bar—just Coca Cola, no booze. I noticed a number of people there with Boston accents. I said, "You guys here for Soupy?" "No, no," they said. They said there was a young comedian from Boston, and they wanted to see what he was like.

In a short time this guy apppeared on stage and said, "I just wrote a song I dedicated to Ted Kennedy. Want to hear it?"

"Yeah!" said the crowd.

"Well, here goes," said the comedian.

"Well, your brother is dead and your brother is dead and your father is dead and your brother is dead, and you killed a girl on the bridge."

I thought it was going to be a 9-1-1 moment. Some of the Boston guys tried to run the stage. I tried to get real small under the bar.

Soupy went on late. I was still there.

11

MOTHERS GOOD AND BAD

Part 1
GOOD MOTHERS:
HONOR THY FATHER BUT NEVER
MESS WITH A MOTHER ON A MISSION

KATHY ODELL

I first met Kathy Odell at an American University dormitory; she was there to pack up her son's room. I was there to cover a fatal hit and run. Her son was the victim.

She said "When I got that phone call, it took my breath away. It was like the life you knew, in that one moment, changed forever."

Thursday, January 28, 1999, Voorheesville, New York. Kathy Odell had just returned to her home from a kickboxing class at the gym. It was around 8:30 at night when she got a call from an emergency-room doctor at Georgetown University Hospital. The grim news: Her son had been the victim of a hit-and-run accident. He was dead.

Kathy Odell loved her son more than anything else in this world. A divorced third-grade teacher, Kathy was not wealthy, but when it came to her son, Matt, her budget was open-ended. Matt was fascinated by the law and politics. Other kids would play ball and listen to music. Matt Odell would watch CNN and C-SPAN. He was obsessed with Washington, and, so, when it came time for college Matt chose American University. It was expensive, but he got some help, and Kathy gathered together the rest of the money needed to send Matt to AU.

When Matt got to Washington, he was all business. At school he chose to live in Hughes Hall on the edge of campus so he could be far away from the Delta House distractions of college life.

Matt Odell was in Washington. He was happy. Kathy was happy. Until that January night. Matt and his friend Jeremy went to a nearby Mini Mart to get a phone card. Both boys were on roller blades. Jeremy heard some engine noise behind him and quickly jumped to the curb, but Matt didn't make it. The truck struck him. The driver didn't stop. The accident occurred on Nebraska Avenue, Northwest, about 100 yards from AU. Matt was taken to Georgetown University Hospital but didn't survive. It was a fatal case of hit-and-run, a matter for the police.

In many ways the police department works like a deli counter. If you are on duty when something bad happens, you have to handle the order – it becomes your case. The death of Matt Odell—the case of his hit-

and-run death—fell into the hands of Detective Milton James, an investigator not easily confused with Sherlock Holmes.

Hit-and run cases are often difficult to solve. If there is no security-camera video, eyewitness, or license-plate number, police have little to go on. In this case, there was no video or license plate number, but there was an eyewitness. There was also a less-than-ambitious investigator who ignored the eyewitness, which almost guaranteed an ice-cold case. Kathy Odell would not let that happen.

A few days after the funeral services for her son in New York, Kathy drove to Washington DC to attend a memorial service for her son. "It was tough—it was like burying him twice," she told me. "I got to meet the EMTs who treated him on the scene. And it was a God-awful scene."

You see, Kathy Odell was, herself, a volunteer EMT. She wanted all the details. She said, "He had to have known he was hit. They suctioned off some of his brain tissue at the scene. For a long time that bothered me."

After the memorial service, Kathy met with Detective James. She sensed something was wrong. "He didn't seem motivated."

Shortly after the accident, police saw a pickup truck with a dented front end and a shattered windshield parked on MacArthur Boulevard, a couple miles from AU. The truck was registered to Shane DeLeon, a carpenter and a friend of a woman lawyer who lived nearby.

DeLeon had a suspended license and a prior drunk-driving arrest. On the night of the accident he had been at a bar called Babe's in Tenleytown. The bartender remembers serving DeLeon that night because he ran out on the tab. For those not familiar with the area, Nebraska Avenue was the most logical route between the bar and the house on MacArthur Boulevard.

To a layperson, this would have appeared to be a simple case. The police had the vehicle; they had their man.

Case closed? Not so fast.

The police didn't submit the DNA samples and other evidence they took from DeLeon's truck to the lab for weeks after the accident because of what the police described later as an "administrative lapse." Jeremy, the only real witness to the crash, said that when he tried to talk to Detective James, the detective cut him off. Jeremy told the *Washington Post* that months went by and no one from the police department called him back.

Kathy Odell went on the warpath. "It became clear early on that they didn't know what they were doing," she said. Kathy worked the case. She called the police with a straightforward message: "If I don't get another detective on the case by six o'clock, I'm going public with all of this."

A new detective was assigned to the case, after which Shane DeLeon arrested and charged with second-degree murder.

Kathy Odell thought finally she would get justice.

Not exactly.

The trial was bizarre. By some press accounts the jury was out of control. Some of the jurors showed up late for court. Some yawned loudly or laughed during key testimony. If that weren't bad enough, during deliberations a fistfight almost broke out.

It was all about juror number nine.

This is how *Washington Post* reporter Neely Tucker told the story: On the vote, 10 of the 12 jurors voted to convict DeLeon of second-degree murder. Not juror number nine. On the next vote, 11 of 12 voted to convict him of a lesser charge: involuntary manslaughter. Not juror number nine.

"You're an ass," the foreman told juror number nine.

"Your mom's an ass," juror number nine shot back.

The two men started at each other. Some jurors ran from the room; others tried to break it up. Later, some of the jurors said they were frightened of juror number nine, fearful that he might hunt them down and hurt them.

After days of arguing and fighting, the jury voted to convict Shane DeLeon of negligent homicide. It was the least of all the charges he faced. Had DeLeon been convicted of second-degree murder, his prison sentence could have been from 20 years to life. Five years was the maximum time for negligent homicide. Shane DeLeon sentenced to five years for negligent homicide, plus two years for an escape from a halfway house – just seven years for killing Matt Odell.

One of the jurors told the Post's Tucker: "Tell the boy's parents we are sorry. This was so wrong."

Kathy Odell was devastated: "In the end, the justice system that my son Matt loved, failed him."

Eventually Kathy Odell found, in the parole system, the justice she was denied in the courtroom. Every time Shane DeLeon came up for parole, she was there to oppose his release. She did it in Washington. She did it in Virginia. She did it in North Carolina.

"He showed no remorse," Kathy said. "He had an attitude. If you asked him, he would say he didn't do anything wrong. He just thought my son was a bag of trash left in the road."

SUSAN LEVY

Chandra Levy is Missing

It was quite a spectacle, this neatly dressed woman walking through town cradling a stuffed yellow duck. She'd come to Washington with a single message: "I just want my daughter back." Her daughter, Chandra Levy, vanished around May 1, 2001. That duck had been one of Chandra's favorite stuffed animals. Susan Levy was on a pilgrimage to find out what happened to her daughter, and I followed her just about every step of the way.

Chandra, an attractive 24-year-old woman from Modesto, California, had been an intern with the Federal Bureau of Prisons as part of a study program to earn her master's degree from the University of Southern California. She was getting ready to return to California for her graduation ceremony when she went missing.

When an adult is reported missing in Washington DC, it's not exactly all-hands-on-deck for the police. Susan Levy was out to change that. So, with Chandra's toy duck she came to Washington to stir the pot. She hired Billy Martin, a well-known lawyer and former assistant U.S. Attorney; Martin new what buttons to push and what calls to make to get action.

Chandra had talked about having a "secret" friend in Washington. Her mother became a detective. Searching her daughter's phone records, she found a number that Chandra had called frequently. That number belonged to Gary Condit, a fifth-term Congressman representing California's 18th Congressional District, which included Modesto. Chandra had met Condit on a tour of the Capitol.

Condit was 28 years older than Chandra., He was married, and a father. Condit denied having anything to do with Chandra's disappearance. In fact, early on, the congressman and some members of his staff denied that he had a relationship with the 24-year-old intern. Susan Levy was Skeptical—with a capital S. Once Condit and Chandra were publicly linked as "friends," the action became fast and furious.

Chandra's missing-person case morphed into a full-fledged criminal investigation. There were interviews and searches, more interviews and more searches. This was a time when cable-news stations were feeling their oats. They fed off scandal and controversy, and the Chandra Levy story was right in their wheelhouse. There were endless stories about Condit's comings and goings and even some about his other relationships. Reporters and cameras followed

Condit everywhere. He repeatedly denied having a sexual relationship with Chandra or anything to do with her disappearance.

Representative Condit hired Abbe Lowell, a well-known defense attorney, to represent him. Lowell said his client passed a privately administered polygraph test in an effort to clear his name. In a national TV interview with Connie Chung, Condit said he was not in love with Chandra, that he was not leaving his wife, and that he would not discuss whether he had a sexual relationship with Chandra out of respect for the Levy family. Condit was not named as a suspect in the Levy case and was eventually cleared as a suspect in Chandra's disappearance.

Susan Levy was not getting the answers she wanted.

In a search of Chandra's apartment, investigators found what appeared to be her last entry on her computer, a link to Rock Creek Park, a 1,700-acre woodland laced with trails and paths. Rock Creek Park is popular with joggers, bikers, walkers, and nature lovers. There was speculation that Chandra might have gone to the Park for a run, but Chandra was not known to be an outdoors runner. She could have gone to the Park to meet someone. Or maybe, God forbid, someone could have taken her there against her will. Rumors running rampant, the cable channels abuzz with speculation.

Police conducted not one but two searches of the Park. They used dogs and cadets and special-ops cops deployed in what appeared to be a strategic search of the place where they thought Chandra might have gone. They found nothing.

What happened to Chandra Levy? Throughout the summer of 2001, Chandra Levy's story was in the news every day – in the papers, on the television – and everyday Susan Levy continued to plead for clues and information, making the tearful plea: "I want my daughter back."

Then on September 11, 2001, the Chandra Levy story went dark as the City and the nation's focus turned to the attacks on the World Trade Centers and the Pentagon. Interviews with Susan Levy cancelled. The gaggle of reporters disappeared from outside Condit's office.

Chandra's Body is Found

On May 22, 2002, a man who routinely walked Rock Creek Park with his dog, Paco, found Chandra Levy's remains in a forested area along a steep incline, an area the police had not searched before. Actually, Paco found the remains. The man walked out of the Park to a nearby construction site and called the police.

We heard calls to the Park Police, the DC police, the FBI, and the the DC Police Chief unfold on the police radio. There were enough cops at the scene to have a union meeting. No one was talking. There was police tape and law enforcement officers moving about behind it, searching. There were conversations but none that we could hear. I thought it had to be Chandra for whom they were searching.

I was the first reporter on the scene, but we had a problem getting on air. I actually did the story first on cable television for MSNBC before I had a chance to do it for News 4. It was Frustrating with a Capital F. I think I threw something or said something—it was not a happy moment. There is nothing worse than having a big story and not being able to tell it.

As with many stories, eventually the facts oozed out, and we later learned that dental records confirmed that the body in the Park was that of Chandra Levy. Her bones and clothing—leggings knotted at the bottom, a sports bra, a sweat shirt, and tennis shoes – were scattered but not buried in the forested area.

The medical examiner declared Chandra's death a case of homicide, saying she was likely choked or strangled.

The Suspect

In September, 2001, a number of signs pointed to Ingmar Guandique, an illegal immigrant from El Salvador, as a suspect in Chandra's murder. He admitted to having assaulted two other women in Rock Creek Park. It was said that he choked them but they managed to escape. He didn't go to work on the day Levy disappeared, and his landlady recalled that his face appeared scratched and bruised around then. Nevertheless, investigators did not interview the women whom Guandique assaulted, and police referred to Guandique only as a person of interest and not a suspect.

Finally, on March 3, 2009, the DC Superior Court issued an arrest warrant for Guandique, who was in prison for his assaults on the two women in Rock Creek Park. On November 22, 2010, the jury found Guandique guilty of the first degree murder of Chandra Levy, and on February 11, 2011 – almost ten years after Chandra's murder – he was sentenced to 60 years in prison. Why did it take so long? How did it come about?

Simply, early on the prosecutors didn't have sufficient evidence to support a conviction.

Enter Armando "The Rat" Morales, the prosecution's secret weapon. Morales, a jail mate of Guandique, testified that Guandique told him he'd attacked Chandra. When Morales took the stand, his testimony was spellbinding. He began by telling jailhouse stories about survival behind bars. It was mesmerizing. Once he established his jail cred, Morales went on to talk about Guandique and how he went after Chandra, saying Guandique didn't know if he'd killed her. Morales's testimony sealed the deal. Guandique was convicted of murder. Susan Levy was there for the trial. She thought justice had been done.

In 2015, Guandique was granted a new trial after evidence surfaced that Morales, the prosecution's star witness, had perjured himself on the stand, that the DNA evidence on Chandra's bra which the prosecution submitted into evidence belonged not to Guandique but to one of the scientists testing it, and that the prosecution had withheld documents from the defense during the trial.

On July 28, 2016, the government announced that it would not re-try Guandique but would, instead, seek to have him deported. After losing his bid to remain in the U.S., Guandique was deported to El Salvador in 2017.

So did Ingmar Guandique kill Chandra Levy? Maybe, but no one has proven it.

JACKIE WINBORNE

Winborne's story is a lot shorter than Susan Levy's because her daughter's case did not gain as much attention as Chandra Levy's. Perhaps that was because her daughter did not have an affair with a Congressman. Perhaps it was because Jackie Winborne was black. Make no mistake about Jackie Winborne, though: She was relentless.

Now to the beginning.

Jackie Winborne had a 23-year-old daughter, Shaquita Bell, who had three children – Ashley, 5; Devontae, 3; and Alexis, 3 months. She was last seen June 27, 1996. At the time of her disappearance she was living in Alexandria, Virginia.

Jackie called Shaquita's ex-boyfriend, Michael Dickerson. Dickerson gave Jackie two different stories: he had dropped Shaquita off on Minnesota Avenue; and Shaquita had called a cab and left in it. He said he was looking for Shaquita.

Sure, he was.

Shaquita's father called Dickerson's father, and Dickerson's father reportedly said, "Call the police and expect the worst."

In the 1990's Dickerson was a drug dealer. When Sean Thomas and a friend attempted to rob some drug dealers in his territory, Dickerson shot and killed Thomas. At the time, Shaquita and Dickerson were living together.

A short time before she disappeared, Shaquita reported to the police that Dickerson had beaten her and threatened her with a gun. She filed assault charges against him. She also told the police that she had overheard him talking about the murder of Sean Thomas. By this time, Shaquita was no longer living with Dickerson.

On June 13, the police picked Dickerson up, found a handgun in his car, questioned him about the Thomas murder, and released him. Two weeks later, Shaquita went missing.

This should have been an easy case, but it lingered, and Jackie Winborne was determined to move it along. She searched for her daughter's body, even digging in the woods with garden tools. Jackie organized demonstrations, created posters: "What happened to Shaquita Bell?" She did TV interviews, radio interviews, everything but take out an ad in the Washington Post.

In 1997, Dickerson was convicted of assaulting Shaquita and sentenced to 15 years in prison.

After her disappearance, Shaquita's purse was found in Jonathan Shields' car. Shields was a friend of Dickerson. Shields told the police that Dickerson said he had killed Shaquita in DC and had asked Shields to help him bury her body. Shields also told the police that Dickerson and he took Shaquita's body to a wooded area along Old Fort Road in Fort Washington, Maryland. In 1999, Shields was not-so-mysteriously killed – before he could further assist the police or testify against Dickerson.

Jackie Winborne organized a protest in front of police headquarters, the message clear: find Shaquita. Police Chief Cathy Lanier said she rarely watched television news, but that day, when she was home with her mother, she walked past the TV and saw Jackie Winborne making a plea: "If I could only meet with Chief Lanier, it would be a blessing for our case."

Lanier said, "Who is this woman and how come I haven't heard about this case before?" At this point, Shaquita had been missing 11 years. On July 4, 2007, Lanier had a face-to-face meeting with Jackie Winborne and made a pledge: "I'm here until we solve this."

Lanier put on a full-court press. She assigned new detectives to the case.

In January 2008, Dickerson was charged with the murders of Shaquita Bell and Sean A. Thomas. In October of that year, he entered a guilty plea to the second-degree murder of Shaquita. In his plea agreement, Dickerson admitted to killing Thomas and agreed to lead the police to Shaquita's grave in exchange for the prosecutor's agreement not to prosecute him for Thomas' murder. Dickerson led police to a stretch of woods in Ft. Washington, Maryland. It was there he said that where he said he buried Shaquita's body. The police searched the area but did not find it.

Dickerson is now serving a sentence of 15 years without the possibility of parole.

Jackie fought for years to find justice for her daughter but never found her body. In 2016, she began a fight for her own life after she was diagnosed with a rare form of cancer.

Part 2

BAD MOTHERS

BANITA MARIA JACKS

In the course of a workday I get all kinds of calls from all sorts of people—all kinds of ideas, tips, suggestions, stories. Many of the calls never pan out. Then there are the calls from sources—people in the know, people who are "All Stars." Eight out of ten times their calls are right on the mark. Big stories—stories that make your palms sweat. When you see an All Star's number flashing on your phone, you stop everything and take the call. There are very good chances that there's something big on the other end.

So it was one day in January 2008. "Get to the 4200 block of Sixth Street, Southeast," he said. "I've never seen anything like this.".

By the time I arrived, the police had blocked the street off. There were knots of cops inside the police tape and knots of neighbors outside. There was an eerie sense of quiet, whispers from both sides. Something wrong, terribly wrong, had happened.

Sometimes it takes time for the truth to ooze out. This was one of those times.

There was, on that block, a red brick row house on a hill. Inside that row house police had found the decomposing bodies of four young girls, all sisters, in one bedroom. Three little girls were lined up in a row, dressed only in white T-shirts. In another bedroom their older teenage sister was lying naked on the floor, beneath her a white T-shirt stained in blood. The four victims had been there for months.

Marshals had made the discovery when they came to evict the family. They smelled a foul odor and traced it to the rotting bodies on the second floor.

Dead were Tatianna, 11; N'Kiah, 6; Aja, 5; and Brittany, 17.

All had been stabbed to death.

Alive and in the house and also dressed in just a white T-shirt was Banita Jacks, the girls' mother.

She told police the girls were possessed by demons and were trying to make her suffer. She said the oldest one, Brittany, was Jezebel, and that she had to keep her locked up to control her. Banita told police she had to get rid of all her furniture because it gave the demons something to hold onto. She said she tossed all the furniture in the back yard. She said she got rid of the girls' clothes and just gave them T-shirts to wear. She said the spirits and demons all have different smells and they would come and contaminate the clothes.

Banita never admitted to killing her children. She said they died in their sleep. When it came time for her trial, she resisted an insanity defense.

Banita Jacks found guilty of murder and sentenced to 120 years in prison. At her sentencing the judge said the gruesome nature of the case would haunt him the rest of his life.

At one time Banita was a hairdresser, a stylist. She grew up in Charles County, Maryland, and dropped out of school in the tenth grade after she became pregnant with Brittany. She moved from place to place before ending up in that house on Sixth Street. Neighbors say that the girls were always clean and well dressed, sometimes with bows in their hair until—well, until her companion, Nathaniel Fogle, died in February 2017. Then, they say, things went downhill. She locked her children in their rooms and denied them food.

Some neighbors recall smelling a foul odor as they walked past Banita's row house in the summer of 2007 but said they believed it came from some sort of dead animal. Social workers who were supposed to check on Banita and her children were faulted for not making the inspections that could have changed the outcome here. Banita's family sued the city. Fingers were pointing in every direction—and there was enough blame and guilt and shame for everyone to share.

RENEE BOWMAN

Nine months after the discovery of the girls in the house on Sixth Street, Southeast, I got another phone call that led me to an unbelievable find in the Town of Lusby, Maryland. It is in rural St. Mary's County about 40 miles outside Washington DC. A neighbor there had spotted a young girl about seven years old, half naked, covered in blood and fecal matter, wandering about the streets of this bedroom community. She had jumped from a second-floor window to escape what turned out to be a house of horror. The neighbor called the cops, who searched the house and inside found a chest freezer—and inside that chest freezer, the bodies of two young girls: Minnet, 10, and Jasmine, 9.

They were special-needs kids. Renee Bowman adopted them, killed them, and kept their bodies in a freezer for about a year and a half as she moved from house to house to house, first in Montgomery County, then in Charles County, and finally in St. Mary's County, where that little seven-year-old girl made her getaway.

The girls' bodies were frozen solid—so ice-cold they had to be kept in a room for several days to defrost before autopsies could be performed. Though they were found in St. Mary's County, prosecutors had to determine the cause of death and the time of death to determine where to try the case. Packaged meat provided the clue. Time-stamped frozen meat from a supermarket in Montgomery County, Maryland had become entwined with the girls' bodies. Montgomery County owned the case.

The star witness: the surviving girl whose identity was protected. The question was whether a girl only seven years old was capable of testifying before a jury. To put her to the test, prosecutor John McCarthy had her read the book *The Pigeon That Drove the Bus* the next day in court in front of the judge. McCarthy asked the little girl what the book was about. She recited the story almost word for word.

On the day of her testimony the little girl came to court dressed in a red jumper. She was holding a stuffed white teddy bear with a red heart. She was too small to be seated in the witness stand, so she stood, and prosecutor McCarthy sat in a chair in front of her and in a skilled and gentle way went through the horrific story of torture and fear.

She pointed to the teddy bear to show where Bowman had beaten her on her backside and between her legs.

She said Bowman kept them locked in a room and made them go to the bathroom in a bucket.

She said Bowman choked her so many times she couldn't count.

She said Bowman used a bat and shoes to beat her.

She said that when she asked Bowman why her sisters weren't around anymore, Bowman told her that her sisters thought she was stupid and went off to live with someone else.

"I can't call her mother anymore," the little girl said.

"What do you call her?" the lawyer asked.

"Ex-mother."

Prosecutor McCarthy argued that Bowman was motivated by money. She received more than $150,000 from the government for taking care of the special-needs kids, much of that money coming after the two girls were already dead and on ice. As this was going on, Bowman was trying to adopt even more children. Her adoption conditions were simple: there had to be support payments and there could be no home inspections.

The jury deliberated for less than two hours to find Renee Bowman guilty of murder. She was sentenced to two life terms in prison.

Plus 75 years. Just to make sure.

12

ON THE ROAD

CROSS COUNTRY

Back in the '70s—back before satellite trucks, back before live views, back before iPhones, back during the energy crisis when gas was rationed, drivers with odd tag numbers filling tanks on odd-numbered days, even tag numbers on even-numbered days—way back then, Channel 9 sent me cross-country to see how the energy crisis was affecting America—a challenge that turned into a trip of a lifetime.

Cameraman Frank McDermott, soundman DJ, and I took off from Washington and headed west in a Volkswagen bus. We had a system:

Drive about 250 miles.

Set up a story for the next day.

Shoot the story.

Write the script for the story.

Record the script in the field.

Drive to the airport.

Fly the story to Washington, counter-to-counter.

And then repeat, repeat, repeat, repeat.

This went on for about three weeks. We never missed a day. We gained incredible insight into life in America.

In Ohio, we found a gigantic mountain of tires and the man who collected them. He said he could extract oil from the old tires and then repurpose the oil. I don't know if it ever worked, but the enormous mound of tires reaching high into the sky was a sight to behold.

In Illinois, we spoke with a farmer and saw huge, gas-powered water sprinklers that looked like spiders on steroids creeping about the field watering his crops. He rationed water to save on fuel costs. Delicate balance: Keep crops alive, keep fuel costs down.

At the Grand Canyon, we interviewed families camping out in RV parks. They talked about how the cost of topping off those gas-guzzling homes-on-wheels affected the enjoyment of their vacations.

The road is the only real way to appreciate the beauty of our country. At the Grand Canyon, though, we took to the air, hiring a helicopter to fly down to the base and then climb up the side. I felt like my nose was going to rub against the Canyon's walls. Goose bumps.

In Amarillo, Texas, we went behind the scene at a cattle auction where ranchers talked about the pain, they felt from the energy crisis. You might say they had a big stake in it. And we couldn't leave without having a steak of our own. It filled the plate.

In Gallup, New Mexico, we had a up-close look at a strip mine. I stood next to one of the claw-like shoveling machines, the tires well over my head. It was the kind of thing you'd expect to see in some monster sci-fi movie scratching deep into the ground. More goose bumps.

In the mountains there were times I thought I was going to have to get out and push that little VW bus to make it to the top, but we made it to Las Vegas and then on to LA, where we left the bus and flew home. Many stories, many memories.

In the long-distance counter-to-counter age of TV journalism, it was quite an experience.

THE WASHINGTON FOOTBALL TEAM

If you are a Dallas Cowboys fan this might be a good time for you to move on to the next story.

It is not now, but for a long time Washington DC was a one-team town. Sure, we had an NBA team. Sure, we had an NHL team and a baseball team. But the WFT was the team everybody cared about. Whites, Blacks, Democrats, Republicans, Catholics, Protestants – most everyone followed the WFT. Through quarterback controversies, Billy versus Sonny, the Hogs, the Hogettes, Charlie Taylor, Art Monk, Larry Brown, John Riggins, the vibrating stands at RFK Stadium were, for decades, a glorious Sunday ritual. When the WFT won on Sunday, on Monday everything would be right. When the WFT lost on Sunday, on Monday everything would be wrong. I say this for younger people who weren't around to experience the glory years of the hometown team.

It's been nearly 30 years since the WFT went to a Super Bowl. When the WFT went to Super Bowls, local television stations would send a task force of reporters, cameramen, editors, and anchors to memorialize the team's every move, talk to fans, take in the action, and broadcast it all live to the people back home. Super Bowls are big fun. They are a lot more fun when your team wins. I was lucky enough to go to three.

Tampa 1984. Not anything I could say or do could help our WFT in Tampa when they played the Oakland Raiders. I had what I called a 'secret weapon' to help the WFT win the game. When I went to Tampa, it went with me in a cylinder handcuffed around my wrist. What was this secret weapon? It was a picture of Hall of Fame coach George Allen. On the night before the game I hung the picture above the lobby overlooking the Raiders' hotel. It didn't work. The game was over at halftime: Raiders 38, WFT 9.

San Diego 1988. A much better time, much better weather, much better result. At every Super Bowl there is a press day where reporters huddle with players at various stations around the stadium asking all sorts of questions. It's a circus. To have some fun I decided to cover it like Barbara Walters and ask players, "If you were a tree, what tree would you be?" It was meant to be a goof on the insane media scrum.

The Washington Football Team won big time: WFT 42, Denver Broncos 10. Dexter Manley was interviewed on network television. The interviewer asked him, "What was the dumbest thing that happened to you at the Super Bowl?" Dexter said, "Some reporter asked me what tree I wanted to be." For the record, I think Dexter said he would have been an oak.

There is a postscript to my San Diego experience: I got a team-autographed ball—not one processed in an autograph machine but one that was passed around and signed by the players. I brought it home and put it on a shelf in the living room. A few months later my kids took it outside to play catch. So much for souvenirs.

Minnesota 1992. Why would anyone schedule a Super Bowl in the winter in a city like Minneapolis? The average winter temperature there: 28 degrees. No shorts, no flip-flops—long johns and down vests. But it was a Super Bowl, so quit whining. The game was played inside the Metrodome, but most of the pre-game activities were outside. I played golf in the snow. There was an ice sculpture wearing a Vikings Helga hat. It was cold—but the people in Minneapolis were warm-hearted and good sports. And it helped a lot that Washington won the game—WFT 37, Buffalo Bills 24.

By the way, there were no trees at that game.

THE OLYMPICS

I have been to the Olympic Games six times. The station sent me not for the sports but to cover lifestyles and action. Every time I went to the Olympics I would do a "souvenir of the day," a "phrase of the day," a "food item of the day," – effective ways to point out cultural differences, not just overseas but in different U.S. cities and States. These are a few of my Olympic memories.

1980 Lake Placid Winter Olympics. The games were on ABC; I worked for a CBS affiliate, which sent me to the games. Winter Olympics attract a wealthy crowd. It takes a lot of money to participate in these games; most of the athletes either come from money or have monied backers. It's the way of the world. I remember seeing a lot of fur coats. I remember people worrying that it might be too warm for some of the events. We managed to buy tickets and shoot many competitions.

Some of the action came and went in a matter of seconds. Take the luge. We could only see part of the race, and before we knew it, the competition was over. People in Lake Placid drive on lakes without fear; they know ice. I did also but reluctantly; I don't know ice. I went to the US-Russia hockey game. It was the Miracle on Ice: USA 4, Russia 3. Holy Cow! No one expected it. Everyone celebrated it. We hopped into an ABC limo that took us to a big after-party that went on forever. God bless Mike Eruzione. God bless ABC.

Los Angeles 1984 Summer Olympics. Many of the events were miles apart from others. I looked forward to the trip, anticipating good weather and good accommodations. Before I left for LA, I was booked into a motel. Imagine my surprise when I arrived to a motel surrounded by a barbed-wire fence. There was no air conditioning and no television, but there was green scum on the pool. I moved to a bungalow in Santa Monica. Granted, I spent a lot of time in traffic, but it was worth it. I tried surfing and quickly discovered that I had no future riding the waves. You might ask why. Well, it was my time up on the board – on my feet. One or two seconds. Maybe four seconds one time – maybe.

Barcelona 1992 Summer Olympics. Barcelona was gorgeous. The venues were gorgeous. The architecture was spectacular. Gaudi's Basilica of the Sagrada Familia is a good example. Construction was started in 1882. I understand it is supposed to be completed in 2025. Even in its uncompleted state, it was spectacular. The food was delicious – the tapas, the rich hot chocolate even in summer. The women were beautiful and flirtatious. We walked the Ramblas—there were birds, street performers, something to see everywhere along the street. Then there was our basketball Dream Team – it beat Croatia in the finals and brought home a gold medal.

Atlanta 1996 Summer Olympics. Hotlanta! How many Peach Streets can one city have? Almost every night there were famous acts, like James Brown and Carlos Santana. Atlanta is close to DC and a lot of Channel 4 viewers told us they planned to attend the games. I wanted to be able to talk with them there. I had a carpenter at the station make a big red number 4 mounted on a pole, and when we went live from Centennial Park, my producer hoisted it up so people from Washington could find us and we could talk to them live on the air. It worked very well until the pipe bomb attack in the park. The fun stopped there.

Sydney 2000 Summer Olympics. Our winter, their summer. I needed two watches to keep track of the time. No Bloomin' Onions here, but plenty of Victoria Bitter beer and Vegemite. We stayed in an old mental hospital. I loved the Aussies, loved to hear them talk. "G' Day, mate!" By the way, a koala bear isn't a bear. But you probably already knew that.

Salt Lake City 2002 Winter Olympics. The acoustics of the Mormon Tabernacle are so perfect that you can hear a pin drop. Young brides line up outside to be photographed in front of the iconic building. We ate lime Jello and rode a train pulled by a steam-engine. There is a Great Salt Lake and we found a pink flamingo there, but Salt Lake City is dry. To get a drink, we had to join a club and order booze an ounce at a time. It was a process, but it worked. We found that strip clubs had a five-foot rule: To tip a dancer you had to wad up the bill and toss it onto the stage. Alcohol and strip clubs aside, the Mormons weren't stuffy. In fact, they were relaxed and most welcoming. I even bought a Latter-Day Saints CTR (Choose The Right) ring. It's a sort of Mormon version of What Would Jesus Do?

13

VANCE

Ron Minor talking about Vance at the Ben's Chili Bowl mural

I knew he had cancer, but for some reason, I thought he would never die. If anybody could beat this, I figured, it would be Vance.

For 48 years, Jim Vance was THE anchor at NBC4 in Washington DC. He was a man's man. He loved to fish. He loved to hunt. He loved to ride motorcycles. He loved sports. And he loved the city of Washington. He was as comfortable talking to presidents as he was hanging out with the guys on the corner.

In many ways Vance was the soul of the City. He guided us through troubled times and celebrated City triumphs. And man, could he tell a story. He had a strong, smooth voice, and when Vance looked into a camera lens—poetry.

Vance traveled far and wide to cover stories, but he did his best work here at home. When violence flared in our city, Vance was there. During terrorist attacks, Vance was there. For the inauguration of seven presidents, Vance was there. He spoke openly about his struggles with drug addiction—twice he battled those demons. In the end, Vance was victorious. Without fanfare Vance raised scholarship money for John Carroll, a difference-making high school in Northeast Washington. Without fanfare Vance counseled young reporters and writers trying to launch careers in the television business. Vance—a force on and off the air.

Just about everything I have written so far are things fairly well known and documented about Jim Vance. I wanted you to know more, so I enlisted the help of some people who had different kinds of relationships with Vance.

Sharon Donnell.

Sharon was Vance's writer for 22 years. She knew his voice.

"Every woman of my generation who works behind the scenes in television news has Mary Tyler Moore to thank. Most of my friends wanted to be Mary Richards, a news producer throwing her hat in the air, exhilarated by the thrill of realizing she was 'gonna make it after all'. I wanted to be Murray Slaughter, the show's wisecracking news writer."

"Like Mary and Murray, I've always worked in local news. Before I landed in Washington, I wrote copy for top-flight journalists and Ted Baxter-type buffoons. The worst was an overpaid and underworked former network newsreader. That guy once dressed me down in front of the entire newsroom for using two dots to indicate a pause—rather than three."

"But Jim Vance. One of the first stories I ever wrote for Vance was a kicker for the 11 o'clock news. I handed in the script minutes before the story aired, and the lede went something like this:

'If you are what you eat, will the new BLUE M&Ms make you sad?'"

"When the story ran in the next block, Vance said words to the effect of: 'M&Ms are coming out in a new color. Blue.'

"I checked the script in the computer, and the producer had rewritten the lede. I messaged him, 'So that didn't work?' And he wrote back: 'VANCE ISN'T GOING TO READ THAT. ' "

"And thus, began the odyssey to unlock the mystery shared by any writer or producer who had ever written for Vance. There was an oft-heard refrain: A writer would lean back in her chair, eyes feasting on a freshly minted sentence, read it aloud, and ask everyone in earshot, 'Do you think Vance will say this?'"

"There was an informal, unwritten, partial list of things Vance wouldn't say. No one had the full list, probably not even Vance."

"At the top: anything that sounded like newspeak. For example, 'A Maryland teacher' became 'A teacher in Maryland' because that's how people talk. He would laugh if you wrote 'fled on foot.' He wouldn't say 'plus.' He wouldn't say 'British soldiers.' He wouldn't say the name of Washington's football team."

"He would not say or do any of the things that make it so easy to parody television news. He would not say or do anything he considered stupid or beneath the dignity of the newsroom he'd led since 1969— much to the frustration of more than one news director over the years."

" 'Do you think Vance will say this?' "

"The answer was often no and rarely a definitive yes. Vance was not an anchor who would openly criticize your work. Nor would he change the copy in the computer while reading scripts before the show. You just had to wait and see. When I was new, I would be in the newsroom quaking inside as my stories approached. I'd casually lean a little closer to the television, my pulse accelerating. If he read the story as written—fantastic. If he really sold it—exhilarating. If he slowed down, sometimes pausing for just a second while he rewrote the story in his mind—dismal."

"Over the years I became attuned to the cadence of his delivery, and even if I was still writing and only listening with one ear, my radar would go off anytime I heard him slow down. That was a telltale sign he was about to ad lib on the fly. Another tell that something had gone wrong: As he put his script aside after the story, he would give an extra hard look at it for a beat. Translated, the look meant: 'WTF was that?"

"It was usually not too hard to look at the story—whether I wrote it or not—and figure out where the writer had gone wrong. We all worked hard to avoid those moments. No one wanted to disappoint Vance. We would have walked through fire for him. He never asked us to do anything but take the work as seriously as he did."

"Even now, more than two years after his death, it's a challenge to articulate exactly how much love and respect the man garnered from everyone who ever worked at NBC4 and from the viewers he served for so long."

"I was his field producer for the 2012 Democratic Convention. Every crew there had to build extra time into the schedule to travel from the media workspace to the Convention Hall because of the heavy security. I soon learned our crew had to build in even more additional time because Vance was stopped every few feet by people who wanted to say hello. They ran the gamut from newsmakers to former neighbors to people who felt as if they knew him because they had grown up watching him on television. At one point, a network-news anchor broke away from his entourage to photo-bomb him. Vance chatted with every person and posed for every picture as if he had all the time in the world."

"One of my last interactions with him came in the middle of the newsroom on an ordinary day, and it concerned an ordinary story. My back was to him, and he came bounding up to my desk, loudly saying my name. I turned, pulse accelerating. He pointed a finger at the rundown on my computer screen and said, 'There—that story right there ' I took one look at it and he said, 'I know Sharon Donnell wrote this story.' "

"He meant I'd written the story in his style."

"I think he chose that exact moment to compliment me because my boss was standing right there."

"I said what I always said at moments like that—'I love you, Jim Vance'—and turned back to my writing."

"Inside, I was throwing my hat in the air."

RON MINOR

Ron Minor was an NBC cameraman for many years and a longtime motorcycle sidekick of Vance. Ron is known as "Chop," and Vance and he rode their big, chromed hogs all over the country. Here are some of Chop's memories:

"Vance was a very generous person. He always insisted on picking up the tab when dining out with friends, be it two or 26 people. Besides donating to local charities and schools, Vance's heart could be touched by stories he reported. I recall one day sitting in his office just a couple of days before Christmas, a producer came in with a script for the six o'clock news. A fire had destroyed a house and belongings, including all the kids' Christmas presents. Vance pulled out his checkbook and wrote the family a substantial check to replace the toys in time for Christmas."

"Vance was the only guy I knew who would ride his motorcycle 80 miles an hour smoking a cigarette at the same time. I know this because I was usually alongside him, and the ashes would blow into my face. Vance would laugh. No problem for him."

"One day, while approaching a stop sign, Vance was trying to light a cigarette. He lost his footing, and the bike went down with his wife, Kathy, on the back. No injuries to report—but Kathy gave him hell."

"Quiet as it's kept, Vance really did like people to recognize him. On numerous occasions, when we were out on a story or just hanging out, people would approach me and say, 'Is that Jim Vance?' I'd say, 'No, ' and he would correct me. I recall a time when we were at a gas station and a woman came up and asked, 'Is that Vance?' 'No, ' I said. Vance rushed past me and let the woman know it was indeed him. The lady left with an autographed Washington Post."

"Two of Vance's favorite foods were chocolate cake and my wife Kathy's potato salad. We frequently made sure he had both. One day I let Vance know that Kathy had made his favorite cake and that special potato salad and then told him when we would be home. But when we got there, we found dirty dishes on the table and a note from Vance thanking us for the salad and the cake. He said he would be back the next day. I forgot he'd kept his bike at my house for a while and knew the garage-door entry code."

Now, Vance had an office full of Emmys and other awards, but he was most proud of being included in the mural on the wall of Ben's Chili Bowl, an iconic DC half-smoke eatery on U Street. The people of Washington voted Vance onto the wall, and I remember, shortly before his death, Vance was there for the unveiling. He had lost so much weight from the chemo, his clothes were falling off. His voice was weak and scratchy from the cancer. He told the crowd of fans that when he first came to DC on June 10, 1969, one of the first places he went to eat was Ben's Chili Bowl.

" 'You cannot imagine my joy and my pride when I got word you all had voted poor-ass little old me to sit on Ben's Chili Bowl wall,' Vance said. 'The blessings never stop.' "

I knew Vance had cancer, but for some reason I thought he'd never die.

14

APRIL 30, 2019
PROVIDENCE HOSPITAL DIED TODAY.

Providence Hospital was the oldest general hospital in Washington DC. It was first located in an old, gray Mission-style building at 2nd and D streets, Southeast.

Providence was run by the Daughters of Charity—an order of Catholic women with flying-nun habits. When they gathered together they looked like a gaggle of geese. Their mission: Care for everyone, particularly the poor.

On St. Patrick's Day, my father would dress me as a Leprechaun and take me to visit patients at the hospital

They did it well. During the Civil War they treated wounded soldiers Blue and Gray.

Providence Hospital died today.

It was 158 years old.

For me it is personal.

I was born in Providence Hospital.

My mother died there. She had breast cancer. I visited her every day. It went on for weeks, months—it seemed like forever. In the end she fell into a coma.

In 1956, Providence Hospital moved to a new site in the Brookland section of Northeast Washington close to Catholic University. There was hope that the University would start a medical school. A medical school needs a hospital. But the hope—the wish—for the med school never came to be.

My three children were born at Providence Hospital—Patrick, then Michael, then Salley. I lost Salley's baby picture; she's not happy about it.

My father practiced medicine at Providence Hospital. I went to grade school in the building next door. Often after school I would walk to Providence and wait in the doctors' lounge for a ride home.

On St. Patrick's Day my father dressed me up as a leprechaun and took me around to see all his patients in Providence. Each tour ended with a visit to Sister Felicita, who ran the kitchen. She gave me cake and cookies.

My father died at Providence Hospital. He was making rounds, seeing patients, when he had a heart attack. He was admitted. That night, a second attack took his life. I was out of town when it happened. I've always regretted not being there.I think about it every time I pass by the building.

Providence Hospital died today.

It was 158 years old.

For me it was personal.

15

STUFF LEFT OUT

SOMETIMES JUSTICE IS NOT COLOR BLIND

Elroy was a cop and part-time entrepreneur. He owned a couple of businesses, including a gas station. His girlfriend at the time owned a dress shop on H Street, Northeast. One Saturday afternoon Elroy was painting some shelves purple in a back room of the dress shop when a guy walked into the shop and announced a robbery. Overhearing the demands for money, Elroy reached for his gun on his way to the front and got a drop on the robber. Elroy didn't call 9-1-1; he had a better idea.

He directed the thief to the back room. He ordered him to strip naked, painted his privates purple, and then, in the middle of the afternoon with crowds of shoppers moving up and down H Street, Elroy shoved the naked, purple-endowed robber onto the sidewalk.

I don't know if anyone keeps score of things like this, but I think it was the first act of community policing in the city of Washington.

THE TABLE

Every newsroom has one—that *table* where people put food for general consumption. Maybe it's leftover Halloween candy or tastings from a new restaurant or platters from an upcoming Greek festival. It's truly a moveable feast, a kaleidoscope of calories within arm's reach—and there are a lot of arms in a newsroom.

Before I go any further, I have to tell you about Barbara Harrison, a long-time anchor and reporter at NBC4. Barbara is one of the most generous and kind people I have ever known. For years, she did a Wednesday's Child segment to promote adoptions in the city and she placed more kids in forever families than Father Flanagan.

Barbara has an inviting house, and she throws wonderful parties—special parties, memorable parties. She was having a party and it was on the day of the party that Barbara became a victim of the *table*. You see, Barbara had ordered a custom cake from the Watergate Bakery, a cake that would be the final sweet taste to end a sumptuous evening. Barbara arranged for the cake to be delivered to the station. No problem: she lives nearby. When that cake came to News 4, it somehow made it not to Barbara's desk but to the *table*.

In a matter of seconds—okay, maybe minutes—layers and layers of deliciousness were devoured – gone. By the time Barbara arrived at the station, there was only a ring of icing left on the bottom of the shiny cardboard box. If Barbara was upset she didn't show it.No cake.No problem.Party on.

RITA GREENE

I had an agreement with Rita Greene's family and the hospital. We could photograph Rita lying in her hospital bed from the hallway, but we could not photograph her face as she lay there in bed, eyes open, mouth agape. Our photos sufficed to help us tell Rita Greene's tragic story.

In 1949, Rita Greene moved to DC from her home in Wheeling, West Virginia. She had just graduated from nursing school and been hired to work at Gallinger Municipal Hospital in Southeast Washington. Tuberculosis was rampant in those days; in fact, the hospital had a special ward just for doctors and nurses who contracted the disease. Everyone feared TB, including Rita.

She became a surgical nurse, hoping that she would have less exposure to the disease in the operating room. That turned out not to be so; one of the surgeons had TB. Rita caught it and was treated for it. Just as she was about to be discharged, the doctors wanted to do a procedure to check the health of her lungs. They administered a pain killer. Rita had an allergic reaction. She went into shock. Her heart stopped. Minutes passed before the doctors revived her, and when they did, she was comatose – in a vegetative state.

That was in 1951. Rita remained in that hospital in that state for 40 years. Forty years with round-the-clock nursing. One nurse spent her entire career caring for Rita. In her hospital room were a crucifix and a picture of the Pope, and nurses often wheeled Rita down to the chapel for Mass. When the hospital changed its name to DC General and the building was remodeled, it was all done around Rita Greene.

I did the story on Rita for television back in the seventies. I flew to Wheeling and interviewed her brother. This was back in the days of film, and we had several cans of film to process. The day after I returned from Wheeling, the boss told me he wanted the story on the news that night. I wrote the script, editor Bill Moore furiously spliced the film together, and at the top of the show that night we ran the incredible story of Rita Greene. I did a live voiceover of the track. The director, Ernie Bauer, hit all the cues. It went on for about four minutes, an incredibly emotional story about this incredible woman from West Virginia.

In 1991 Rita's brother arranged for her to be taken back to Wheeling. She died there in 1999. She was 71 years old.

DREAM TEAM

WTOP Channel 9 dominated the Washington DC news for years. Many times its ratings equaled those of all the other local stations combined. Channel 9's anchor team was Gordon Peterson and Max Robinson. Then a couple of things happened. First, Robinson left Channel 9 to anchor the news at ABC. Next came the swap. I talked about this before but it's worth mentioning again because I think it changed the direction of television news in Washington DC. Fearful of FCC intervention, the Washington Post traded WTOP, its station in DC, for WDIV in Detroit, which was owned by the Detroit Evening News.

Because of the swap, there were questions about whether the contracts of some of the Channel 9 reporters and anchors were still binding. Gordon Peterson thought his contract had terminated. NBC offered Peterson a position alongside Jim Vance. Gordon and Jim would be a dream team. They would dominate the ratings for decades. At least that's what NBC and Peterson thought. They struck a deal; Peterson accepted NBC's offer. NBC and Peterson popped Champagne; they held a news conference. They were were ready to go.

Maybe not. The Detroit Daily News, Channel 9's new owner, saw the deal differently. It believed Peterson was still under contract to Channel 9 and had a legal obligation to work there. Channel 9 went to court. There was an ugly summertime trial. Some dirty laundry was exposed. In the end, Gordon Peterson stayed at Channel 9, judge's orders.

Jim Vance went on to have more on-air partners than Elizabeth Taylor had husbands.

Until 1989,

That's when NBC brought Doreen Gentzler to town. And you know what happened after that.

MY PRISON PEN PAL

Before I opened the envelope, I knew the letter was from him. The return address bore his name, Thomas Sweatt, and his address, the federal prison in Terre Haute, Indiana.

Before he took up residence in federal government-provided housing, Thomas Sweatt was a manager of a fast-food restaurant in DC. He was also one of the most famous serial arsonists in Washington DC's history.

For 30 years, someone started hundreds of fires in Washington DC and Prince George County, Maryland. The person who started them seemed to follow no pattern and appeared to have no motive. He set fires in different neighborhoods and at different times of the day. It was an unnerving time in the City

What tied each of the fire scenes together was the incendiary device. The arsonist filled a milk jug with gasoline,

Plugged the opening with a piece of clothing that served as a wick,.

And lit the wick.

The DNA evidence found at two crime scenes linked Thomas Sweatt to the fires. Sweatt was taken into custody after a security camera photographed his car at the scene of a fire near a Marine Corps barracks.

Sweatt pleaded guilty to starting over 400 fires. He had a sexual fascination with men in uniform—Marines, cops, firefighters. He would follow them to their cars or their homes. Then, to get their attention, he would torch the car or the home.

I broke the story on Sweatt's arrest and the DNA clue that led to his capture. Sweatt knew who I was and what I did.

In 2006 I wrote to Sweatt seeking a jailhouse interview. In a neatly printed letter, he replied with a request for a favor. "It's really a small one," he wrote.

"Pictures of firefighters and police cruisers. I don't need the identity of the person, just the bottom— preferably the feet. I have this thing for nice big feet."

He said he wanted the pictures for his album. I thought he wanted them for something else.

I never sent the pictures. I never got the interview.

16

FINAL THOUGHTS

I love my job. As a reporter I have had a front-row seat to tragedy and triumphs. I've seen tears of sadness and heard cheers of joy. I have been fortunate to be a part of what I call the Golden Age of Local Television News.

When I started my career, people in local news forged their own way; there were no footprints to follow. News shows went from a half hour to an hour to an hour-and-a-half to two, then three, and then four hours. As the shows grew longer so did their resources. Local news attracted creative people who were willing to take chances. They were cameramen, reporters, producers – journalistic gunslingers. Everything was new. We tried various storytelling techniques; our bosses encouraged us.

Driving this was a dramatic change in technology. When I started, everything was recorded on film. All film— cameramen used big Aeroflex and Auricon cameras with Bell and Howell winders for cutaways.

Our newsgathering day ended early because we had to allow time to process and edit the film. That process could take more than an hour. Camera magazines held 400 feet of film—three minutes for every 100 feet. A story had to be really good to shoot more than 400 feet. We would shoot silent coverage of hearings, then bring witnesses into the hallway and have them repeat what they said on a sound camera. It a challenge but it saved a lot of precious film.

Over the years I developed a walk-and-talk style of reporting that came as a direct result of working with film. I developed that style working with film on weekends with cameraman Kline Mengle. We would interview the subjects and field track the story walking in and out of frame so that once it came out of the processor we could cut and go. It made for a fast-paced story and a early exit on a Saturday. This technique worked so well I have used it thousands of times.

Now, one quick technical note for the old film people: For the scenes to match up, I would have to repeat the last lines of one before I moved on to the next scene. It was a 28-frame solution. Ask an old cameraman—he'll explain.

Videotape was the game-changer. We could roll and roll and roll some more. We could shoot in low light levels. We could watch the product of our shoots instantaneously. No more processors. No more delays. I think I did one of the first series on videotape. It was about sex doctors, and several dozen couples at a University of Maryland auditorium lying on pasha pillows watching porno films in an experiment to lower their sexual inhibitions. The shooting, no problem. The editing? Different story.

Next came the live truck. It gave TV reporters the ability to go live from a remote location with video and audio, presenting the story from the scene right there in your living room. TV stations couldn't get those trucks fast enough. We went live from birthdays and bar mitzvahs. We went live when a traffic light changed. We went live at murder scenes. We went live during snow storms. When I first worked in a live truck, we didn't have a generator. I had to go to a house, knock on the door, and ask the homeowner if we could plug into the house's outdoor outlet so we could go LIVE.

One of our first big shots from the live truck was down the street from the Channel 9 studio. The scene was an Italian restaurant. My cameraman, Peady Schifflett, looked like an astronaut with a huge camera draped over his shoulder, a fat, cumbersome cable leading back to the truck. Peady weaved his way around tables of diners as I talked to the owner about the wonders of pasta. Okay, it wasn't exactly breaking news, but we were LIVE and Peady didn't die.

There were no cell phones when we first went live from the truck; we communicated through hand-held radios. I knew I was on the air when the cameraman pointed his finger at me. It was primitive—but it worked. Then came cell phones and far more sophisticated ways of moving pictures, sound, and news stories around.

Today we use something called a LiveU or Dejero, essentially a bundle of cell phones that can broadcast live reports from a device about as big as a cake box. It works anywhere you can get a cell signal, which is just about anywhere except some parts of Charles County, Maryland. I used it to go live from London. No more finger-pointing now. Unless I say something wrong.

As technology changed, so have the viewing habits. Stations that used to sign off at midnight now are on 24-7—always there, always on.

Cable added another dimension. Instead of five or six choices to watch with cable there are scores of channels including a number of cable news channels. Controversy drives cable news. Though many of the cable news shows are produced by "news departments," many of the shows themselves are highly opinionated bombastic forums for the right or left. They sometimes bring in legitimate reporters using them to bolster their point of view. I feel sorry for reporters who get forced to participate in that sort of journalistic food fight.

On to the digital age of Twitter, Facebook and citizen journalist. You don't need a license to practice journalism. Anyone can start a blog and call it news. Someone reports something, somebody else picks it up and reports it again and again. And all of a sudden it look like news. But is it? And who is vetting all of this?

Remember, when you were young and played telephone. When a child at the head of a line whispered something – let's call it news---to the child behind him and then each child repeated it on and on and on. By the time the "news" passed through six or ten kids it was hardly recognizable. At a time when many want to be first with the news they are willing to gamble on the accuracy of what they say. Facts and Fairness be damned.

So you have all of this information from all these media sources in a fast-paced gigantic journalistic food processor, churning and spinning in a news cycle moving at the speed of a tweet. And somewhere in the midst of all of that is the truth often bruised and battered.

But as they say, and I hate it when they say it.

"It is what it is"

But it really isn't. Is it?

That's why we really need skilled reporters.

So, go out and find a good story. And ask somebody what they make of it.